Countrywise Two

by

Raymond Rush

Illustrated by

Gavin Clowes

CHURNET VALLEY BOOKS
1 King Street,
Leek, Staffordshire. 01538 399033
email: picture.book@virgin.net web: freespace.virgin.net/c.hinton/

ISBN 1897949 65 0

My Little
Grey "Fergy"

Contents of Countrywise Two

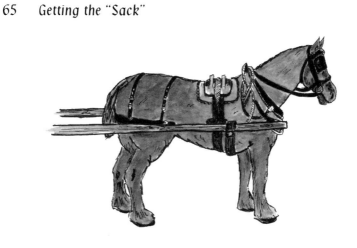

Foreword

After the success of Countrywise One, it was very encouraging to be asked to continue this series. The forty stories in Countrywise Two are a continuation of the previous book, and I am indebted to the past and present editors of 'The Town and Country Post' for allowing me to publish them here.

I am still contributing an article to the same newspaper every month, and the total has now reached two hundred and twenty. This could mean a series of six Countrywise books, and by that time, God willing, I may have written enough for yet another.

A recent reward, derived more from age than ability, has been that after forty-seven years of preaching I have been made 'Reader Emeritus'. It probably means I am past my 'sell by' date, although I still take a church service somewhere every Sunday.

One unexpected upshot of Countrywise One has been an approach by a television producer. The book contains explanations of the origins of many words and I was asked to write a script which included some of them. This was filmed and immediately taken up by Channel 4 who have already asked for a further ten programmes. These short programmes are entitled "What's in a word" - I hope you get a chance to see some of them.

Gavin Clowes has again managed to find enough 'spare' time to illustrate the book for me. His drawings have had to be sandwiched between his hectic life as a schoolteacher, and extracurricular activities with the youngsters like sport, and computer skills, as well as the demands of his own three children's sporting lives.

Raymond Rush
February 2000

Contents of Countrywise One

45 January 1985 Shepherding
HOW THE WILY SHEPHERDS OUTWIT THEIR EWES

To most people the mere mention of the word shepherd conjures up an immediate image of an idyllic life spent sitting in the sunshine idly whiling away the hours. Fleecy white clouds float slowly across an azure blue sky above, and contented sheep gently graze the green grassy slopes of the hillside below where he sits. The melodic music from the continual tinkling of their bells completes a nostalgic picture of pastoral life to delight both the ear and the eye. Although this scene might occasionally have happened, the fact was that most shepherds worked very long hours, frequently in extremely unpleasant climatic conditions. Generally they reared a large family and lived in almost continual poverty. Some relief was often obtained by a illicit poaching. It was for this reason that, on the inside of the shepherd's eight yards of honeycombed drab linen twill smock, were concealed two large poacher's pockets. These would hide any rabbits or hares that he knocked over with his long crook as they squatted in their grass-covered seat or form.

Because the shepherd was away from home for long periods, especially at lambing time, he was provided with a portable four-wheeled hut to live in. It contained a bed, stove, cooking facilities, animal medicines and also a space to warm new born lambs and keep 'cades'. Ewes, having two teats, usually have only sufficient milk to suckle two lambs. When triplets or quadruplets were born the extra lambs had to be bottle fed every two hours. These and orphan lambs were called 'cades'. They caused the shepherd a great deal of extra work so, at the earliest opportunity, they were returned to the flock. But sheep are notorious for refusing to foster any lambs which they do not recognise as their own by sight or smell. They will attack and even kill those confined with them. To overcome this difficulty the shepherd would confuse a labouring ewe by smearing her birth waters on to a cade lamb and present it to her. Thinking it had just been born, she would accept it and start licking it, as well as her own lamb delivered a few moments later.

If a lamb died, another well-tried method was to camouflage the cade lamb's smell by covering it with the dead lamb's fleece, before introducing it to the mourning mother. Sometime a ewe was yoked for two or three days while the cades suckled. When she was released the lamb and its dung would be scented with her characteristic smell and might be accepted. Other cade lambs were fostered by the shepherd's or his neighbour's children, who reared them as family pets.

Until the grass grew, food had either to be carted to the sheep or the sheep folded on the food. If folds were erected, the posts often had to be driven into the frozen ground and posts wouldn't last long if hammers were used. Instead a hole was made with an iron fold pritch or crowbar and the post just tapped home enough to hold it firm. Hurdles were attached on the inside with a loop of string. Moveable wheeled iron hurdles were a later development. Heavily pregnant ewes and newly born lambs were protected from the biting East wind and driving sleet and snow by straw lined hurdles and thatched hurdle roofs.

When folding turnips, the tops and bulbous part was eaten first. To avoid wastage the remaining root had to be grubbed out with a two pronged turnip hack. 'Crones' - old ewes who had lost their teeth - would soon starve on this hard diet, so their roots had to be cut up into manageable portions with a cross shaped chopper or cylindrical slicer, and they were fed separately.

Spring born lambs ran with their mothers until the middle of July, when they were weaned. This was because on the first of August - Lammastide - sheep were allowed on to the aftermath, or eddish, of the hay fields and, from 29th September, they could graze the similar re-growth on the corn stubbles. These periods of time were called Lammas-shack and Michaelmas-shack and the lush feeding flushed the ewes into good condition for breeding. Shepherds wanted lambs at the beginning of April so that they would grow with this grass. This meant that the rams had to be restrained from mating until after Hallowe'en, but the rams wanted to get on with what nature had intended them to do. They had to be restrained and would cause great damage with their strong horns, butting woodwork and walls in their endeavour to break free - causing a proper 'Ramshackle'?

The Celtic way of calculating the gestation period (pregnancy) of the ewes was by using the stars! By noting the position of Daneb, in the constellation of the Swan, at dawn on the day that the rams were turned in with the flock, the first lambs should be born when Vega occupied the same position at sunset - one hundred and forty-three days later.

Contrary to popular belief, although crooks were known by the Saxons, they didn't become fashionable among shepherds until after the dissolution of the monasteries. From then on the crook became the hallmark of the shepherd's trade. Wooden ones were made of ash or hazel, the curved loop being carved from the root - or bent by heat in inferior crooks. Hill shepherds' cromachs used the carved core of a ram's horn fined to a wooden helve or handle. Most English crooks had iron ends, made to the shepherd's requirements by the village blacksmith, the most highly valued being made from old gun barrels. Some crooks caught the sheep by the neck, some were used for pushing the sheep's head under when dipping, but the majority were leg crooks - used just above the hock on the hind leg. The decorative whorl served a useful purpose when digging sheep out of snowdrifts at night, for it was from there that the lantern was hung.

A constant watch always had to be kept for predators and marauding dogs who would panic and savage the pregnant ewes, causing them to abort their lambs. To help guard against such mishaps, the sheep being lost in mist, fog, blizzard, or becoming overlooked by witches, about one in seven had a bell fastened around its neck as an early warning system, and this sheep became known as the "bell wether".. The bells were the prized possessions of the shepherd and were passed down through the generations. The different types had names that sounded as melodic as their many tones - canister, clucket, cup, crotal, rumbler and latten. When the sheep were grazing normally, the bells would emit a low clunking sound, but if the sheep were alarmed, the noise would change into an agitated jangle, immediately putting the shepherd on his guard.

Throughout the ages shepherds have carried some form of protection. In biblical times slings and stones were very accurate weapons, as the shepherd boy David proved when he met the giant Goliath. And most of us know Psalm 23 "The Lord is my shepherd - Thy rod and Thy staff comfort me". The staff, like the mountain shepherd's cromach, was to help him climb the rocky outcrops and test the depth of rivers before fording them. But what was the rod? Well, the rod was to the shepherd what the shillelagh was to the Irishman, the truncheon to the policeman and the rolling pin to the irate housewife - a heavy and effective wooden weapon against interlopers, intruders and husbands who came home intoxicated!

As you probably know a Bishop carries a decorative crook as a symbol that he is the pastoral shepherd of his 'flock'. The correct name for his ecclesiastical crook is a crozier, which reminds me of the story my Dad used to tell about the Bishop who enquired of the shepherd how many sheep he looked after; "About two hundred" came the reply. To which the Bishop replied "I have many thousands". "Blimey" said the shepherd, "I wouldn't care for your job around lambing time!"

46 February Save Our Sacks
SAVE OUR SACKS PLEA FROM DOORMAT TO SUNSHADE......THEIR
USES ARE ENDLESS

*A calf 'bagged-up'
and ready for
transport to
market on the
backseat of my
car. See page 10.*

Over the last few years they have been gradually phased out. We don't have them delivered on to the farm any more and, as a result, they have become very scarce. The few that remain around are quite keenly sought after, especially by we older generation of farmers, who have been brought up to appreciate the multitude of uses to which they can be put. In fact I still use them quite frequently. What are they? SACKS!

Nowadays, most farmers order large consignments of corn, loose and in bulk. Smaller quantities come in paper sacks and fertilisers are purchased in polythene bags of rainbow hues. Yet only a few years ago the hessian sack was the main container for carrying all these items around the countryside. Their uses and mis-uses played an important and interesting role in rural life. Once emptied, the temptation was to throw the discarded sacks into a higgledy-piggledy pile in the corner. There they would soon become infested by rats and mice, who would nibble holes or nest in them and greatly reduce their value, but they did not fancy folded sacks as much.

It was one of the periodic wet weather jobs of yesteryear to sort the dusty sacks into piles according to size. Each pile was then sub-divided into four groups:

1. Plain sacks with no printing on them
2. Those with the merchant's name on them
3. The merchant's name on the outside and another on the inside
4. Dirty, damaged and inferior sacks.

Similar styles of sack were cross-folded in fives, rolled up and bundled into a bag of the same type. When full the sack was tied and a Milk Marketing Board churn label was attached to state how many sacks it contained. It was then hung from the rafters or stored in a vermin proof bin.

The best price for returned sacks was generally obtained from the merchant who supplied them. At each delivery the firm would take back their own sacks to clean and re-use. Their value would be invoiced and deducted from the next bill. There was, however, one drawback. Farm accounts eventually had to go 'under the scrutiny of the taxman'. Returned sacks were classed as income and tax was payable on the money received. One way around this problem was to sell them privately, but this system had its drawbacks. Although bag merchants were usually trustworthy, quite frequently dishonest traders would call at the farm to buy the sacks. Each glib talker had his own method of trying to twist the tally and, as a result, most of us have learned our lesson the hard way - after being diddled out of far more money than we would ever have paid in taxes.

But sacks had many other uses. Grass and clover seed sacks were finely woven and much sought after by thrift conscious country housewives. After they had been washed, a length of linen tape was stitched on to them and fastened around the waist they would make a long, hard-wearing, apron. Others were made into towels or tea towels. They were halved, hemmed and had a loop of tape stitched on to the corner to hang them up after wiping the hands or drying the dishes in the kitchen, back kitchen or wash-house.

A coarse sack was strategically placed just inside the back door to wipe muddy boots and shoes before entering the flag-floored kitchen. The dog lay curled up on another in front of the black leaded grate, as he steamed himself dry after his work outside in the cold and wet. A sack rolled against the bottom of the door excluded floor draughts, and one tacked to the inside of the door frame acted as a curtain to control top draughts. Exposed water pipes were lagged with them in the winter. During summer storms milk churns were stored over night in tanks of cooling water, and they had wet sacks draped over them to reduce the temperature even further to prevent the milk souring.

Before the days of mains water and hosepipes, large gallonages were wheeled in open-topped swinging containers, from wells or streams. To stop the water slopping around and spilling over, a heavy wet sack was laid on top. I used the same method when carting water to my cows in a 300 gallon tank. Two sacks tied side by side on top stopped me getting drenched - unless my tractor had to make an emergency stop at the crossroads!

My grandmother had a mania for collecting old materials, dresses, skirts, stockings and such-like, which she unceremoniously ripped into strips, cut into lengths and stored in a white cotton flour sack. On winter evenings she would sit by the fire, and prod, row after row of the pieces into the sack backing of her peg rug with her special spiked tool. Sacking was also a suitable base for the tapestry of church kneelers and many a bran or sawdust filled hassock owes its origins to the industry of the religious needlewoman - by courtesy of Messrs Silcocks, Bibby or B.O.C.M. (British Oil and Cake Mills).

Casual farmworkers who needed temporary accommodation stuffed a large sack with hay, straw or beech leaves for use as a mattress. At night they would 'hit the sack' and cover themselves with another - as a blanket. If their work was not up to standard, they were given 'the sack' - into which they put their tools and belongings and went on their way to the next farm or hiring fair.

Until regulations forbade the practice, I always took my calves to market on the back seat of my car; with their head protruding from an airy sack, whilst any cow down with milk fever had her back kept warm with a sack blanket. A sack put over an animal's head, when leading it to somewhere strange, would sometimes stop it shying away. This 'dodge' is often used today to help a horse enter its racing stall. To stop hens pecking at their eggs and eating them, sacks were hung in front of the nestboxes to darken them, and broken windows were temporarily repaired by nailing a sack over them.

If the seams of large sacks were un-stitched, the opened bag could be used to carry light, but bulky loads such as loose straw to bed the calves and lawn mowings or autumn leaves to the compost heap. Damaged sacks were cut up to mend others, and many a leaking roof or bucket bottom has been given a new lease of life by tarring the area, applying a patch of sacking and tarring it again on top!

Even today, in wet or wintry weather, I wear a sack over my shoulders. It will soak up a lot of moisture before any seeps through to me. A second sack tied around my middle keeps my waist warm and dry, and, just occasionally, I wear a third - corner tucked inside corner - as a hood. It covers my head, neck, shoulders and back - vulnerable parts?

In late spring I have saved many a border of tender bedding plants from the disastrous effects of a sudden frost by throwing a few lightweight sacks over them. During the haymaking season I bounce along sitting on a sack cushion, which covers my cold metal tractor seat. Another sack hangs in front of the radiator to increase the temperature and allow the engine to run on paraffin instead of the more expensive petrol and, if the sun is shining, I trundle around in the cool under a sunshade, made in a matter of minutes from four bamboo garden canes and a sack - a bit Heath Robinson perhaps, but far cheaper than any purchased tractor cabs.

It's a shame that such a useful item is in danger of becoming extinct. Perhaps I ought to start a campaign to 'Save the Sack'. Then, who knows, I might even 'Get the Sack'.

47 March Childhood Memories
**SIGHTS AND SOUNDS THAT STIR
CHILDHOOD MEMORIES**

Do you sometimes find that a certain word or saying, song or sound, place name or picture will spark off a series of thoughts that you had otherwise completely forgotten, kindling recollections that had remained dormant somewhere in the shadows of your mind until that moment? Mine started a couple of weeks ago, when my wife and I received an invitation to attend my uncle's ninetieth birthday party. He is still farming and he still rides his bike!

I was born on a neighbouring farm at Yaxham in Norfolk and went to the same school as his six children. So this month I would like to share with you some of the sights, sounds and smells that have surfaced since I started recalling my happy childhood memories.

On most mornings I was awakened at first light by our Rhode Island Red rooster, who heralded the dawn from his vantage point on top of the manure midden. At about the same time the wagoner would walk to work, whistling away. He lifted the latches of the split stable doors and soon afterwards he would lead his horses to the farm pit where they would drink long and deep, snorting the water from their nostrils as they did so. In summertime the surface of the pond was frequently speckled with white feathers from the moulting ducks. They gobbled up the tadpoles and fought for possession of frogs that basked in the shallows when the sun was shining.

In a neat nest, built just above water level, the waterhen had reared her brood. At the first sign of danger she would cluck in alarm, twitch her tail and dive overboard. She was immediately followed by all her chicks plopping into the water and swimming in line astern behind her, leaving thin trails through the pond weed as they passed. Each time she gave her warning cluck the white feathers in her tail twitched, teaching the chicks to follow her and retreat out of harm's way, which is why the white feather became the symbol of a coward - but also giving rise to the wise old adage, 'He who turns and runs away, lives to fight another day!'

Meanwhile the horses, their thirst quenched, were re-tied, groomed and given their breakfast of oats, while the wagoner went whistling home for his.

The clanking of the pump handle outside the dairy door meant that my mother was drawing the water for the day. As an aroma of sizzling bacon drifted up the stairs, I dressed and went down to my breakfast of oats - Scotts Porridge Oats - steaming hot with a crusty coating of brown sugar on the top. I poured some milk on to cool it. The milk ran around the edges of the bowl and it lifted the porridge into an imaginary floating island, around which I carved caves and coves with my spoon as I ate. Next came a soft boiled egg. The top removed, I dipped my 'soldier' fingers of bread and butter into the rich golden yolk. Outside a hen cackled to announce that she had just completed her day's work by laying me another for my next breakfast.

The horses whinnied impatiently in their stalls. They stamped and scraped their iron shoes on the stone setts of the stable floor. They were anxious to be harnessed and off, clip-clopping across the cobbles and through the gate that led to the fields.

In the cowshed my father was busy milking. He sat, firmly balanced on the front leg of his three-legged stool, his head tucked tightly into the flank of the Shorthorn cow. The galvanised bucket was wedged securely between his knees and as he squeezed the teats alternately against the palms of his hands, a steady stream of milk streaked into the pail. The harsh, hollow, high-pitched, drumming of the first few squirts that beat against the bottom of the empty bucket gradually reduced in register down the musical scale as the depth of milk increased. It also softened in tone as a layer of froth formed on top!

Each summer an uncle, aunt and cousin from London would spend a fortnight's 'holiday', helping us to bring the harvest home. At least it was a change from their routine of office life. When my uncle came down to breakfast he used to rub the sharp grey stubble of his face against my tender cheeks and make them smart. And I always wondered - why did Auntie wear whiskers on her chin?! And why wasn't she ordered to eat her crusts to make her hair curl like I had to?

In the cornfields the inside of my little arms soon became scratched and sore when helping to stook the prickly corn sheaves and my ankles ran red and raw from walking through the newly cut corn stubbles. They proved even sharper than my uncle's whiskers! When gathering in the corn, how my cousin and I used to love to ride on the horses, or bounce up and down over the ruts in the empty wagon. It was a complete contrast returning home on top of the roped load. All the bumps were absorbed by the layers of ripened sheaves beneath us, and what a long way we could see from those dizzy heights. Gradually the loads of small sheaves grew into large stacks.

In the winter time the stackyard again became the centre of activity, as the thrumming threshing machine separated the sheaves into straw, chaff and grain. There was the added thrill of running after the rats that tried to escape from the ricks. And afterwards in the company of a couple of my older and more courageous cousins, there was the excitement of climbing the long thatching ladder and sliding down from the top of the high straw stack into a deep mattress of threshed straw underneath.

Winter brought the cold winds which lashed hailstones against the window panes, blew the draught-proofing curtains away from the door, moaned down the chimney and sent clouds of smoke billowing into the room. Cracks and crevices around the sash windows were stuffed with newspaper to eliminate the whistling wind, but sometimes even those were dislodged by a sudden gust. In frosty weather the fire in the hearth burned blue. It cast flickering shadows on the walls and ceiling - until the Aladdin lamp was lit. I used to sit entranced on the hearthrug, gazing into the glowing embers of the fire and imagine castles and palaces ever changing in shape, colour and complexity.

Beside me came the contented purring of our old cat Betty, as she lay full length on my father's knee, rhythmically retracting her curved claws. From the opposite side of the fireplace came the constant clicking of knitting needles, as my mother made patches to darn my socks. They had worn thin at the heels and I had made large holes in them rubbing my chilblains!

Soon there were more gigantic ghostly shadows, this time cast by my candle as I crept upstairs, said my prayers and jumped hastily into bed with my hot water bottle. Oh!, the lovely smell that rose from the candle when it was blown out. Just outside my bedroom window the tu-whit-tu-wooing of the owls in the old oak tree made me cringe further under the bedclothes and cuddle tighter to my teddy bear!

There are so many more tales to tell you..... I've been working it out, if I live to be as old as my uncle, I might have room for quite a few more memories, because at my present rate I should have time to write about another 400 articles!

48 April Churchwardens' Duties
A RUDE AWAKENING FOR MEN WHO DOZED OFF IN CHURCH

By tradition, on the Wednesday after Easter, all parishioners are invited to the annual Vestry meeting to elect new Church officers for the following year. Two of the most important vacancies to be filled are those of the churchwardens. Originating before the 14th Century as 'Questmen', or 'Synodsmen', both were initially chosen by the Parish Priest. Since this sometimes led to suspicion and even conflict it was later changed so that one was nominated by the priest and the other by the people. Their present-day duties are to ensure the smooth running of the church, that its services are correctly conducted, that records of baptisms, banns, marriages and burials are entered in the registers by the Priest, together with the number of communicants, the total amounts of collections and any costs incurred. It is their duty to see that the building and contents are kept in good repair and to report any default, defect or disorder to the Archdeacon at his Visitation. To the credit of those concerned, seldom does anything go amiss. Many hold the honorary office for several years at a stretch and perform their duties admirably.

How different from the excessive workload required of them in earlier times! All eligible landowners, tenants, householders and craftsmen were compelled to serve for one year in turn and, if nominated, could be fined up to twenty pounds if they refused. So time-consuming were their tasks that some churches had to enrol four, eight or even twelve wardens! Later some of their ecclesiastical duties were taken over by Sidesmen, Sacristan (Sexton), Verger, Clerk and Beadle, and their civil tasks by Constable, Excisemen, Waywarden and Overseer of the Poor.

What did the churchwarden's job entail? They had to make sure everyone attended church. They visited all houses, ale-houses and inns during divine-service to see that no-one was playing truant. The fine for non-attendance was two pence, unless the person concerned had a good excuse - childbirth, sickness or working, for example as a shepherd. If they rang the bells at 7am it meant Mass or Matins started at 11am and bells at 1.00pm signified a 'Nones' service at 3pm. They tolled the curfew nightly at 8pm in winter and 9pm in summer, to warn people to cover their fires before retiring. The gleaning bell meant you could scour the corn fields for fallen grain and the pudding bell told when the bake ovens were heated. Sometimes, as at St Mary's, Nantwich, the oven was in the church. There the wardens would supervise the weekly baking of the communion bread and the dole rations for the poor.

Because money was scarce, benefactors often gave gifts in kind. The church might even find that it became the owner of the brewhouse. This was especially useful as it enabled the wardens to brew the church ales, held four or five times a year to raise money for repairs to the church.

In many parishes a portion of the glebe land, given by a generous donor, was divided into strips and 'allotted' to workers who had no garden, or wanted an extra patch to grow some corn or vegetables. These small parcels of ground were allotted for two years by the wardens and became known as allotments. If a farmer left a legacy which included animals - sheep were loaned out for three pence a year and milch cows for half a crown. Cottagers who bequeathed hives of honeybees added a sweetness to many a poor person's life before the days of sugar. The beeswax was returned in part payment, so that the wardens could make it into candles to light the church the following year. A yoke of church oxen helped the poor to cultivate their crops cheaply, the charge was one penny a day and included the use of the parish plough, which was usually stored at the back of the church when not in use - as was the Maypole! Beside them hung long grappling irons, ropes and hooks to rip the thatch from burning buildings - it was not uncommon to find the fire engine housed next to the font! Gifts of pots and pans, crockery and cutlery, silver and jewellery, clothing, footwear and furniture all had to be sorted by the wardens and sold at a profit or stored for future use or rental. Many a buxom bride has swept up the aisle to the altar clad in an expensive bridal gown and bedecked with jewellery specially loaned for the occasion by the churchwardens.

Although strictly illegal, the wardens often charged for any 'extras' required by the rich. Candles at christenings and funerals, the processional cross, tapers, pall, cope, censer and hearse. Seven pence if the 'passing bell' was rung at night, or fourpence if during daylight hours. 'Pit' or 'lairstall' money was charged on those buried inside the church, three shillings and four pence (one sixth of a pound) if in the nave and six shillings and eight pence (one third of a pound) in the sanctuary. Because the increasing use of linen was affecting the wool trade it became law in 1667 that all corpses must be laid to rest wrapped only in a woollen shroud. Non-compliance incurred a penalty of five pounds. The cold alternative was to be buried naked! About this time a fine of three shillings and four pence was also imposed on any lady not wearing a woollen cap in church.

The wardens also collected the church tithes - one tenth of all corn, hay, wool and produce. This was stored in the great tithe barns. Later, money was taken in lieu of some items as a special church rate. In 1724 it was two pence per milch cow, a penny a sheep, lambs a half penny, two eggs for every hen and three eggs for every cock, a halfpenny per chimney, a halfpenny per garden, householders and communicants paid a penny per year. From 1697 a window tax of two shillings was collected for up to nine windows and thereafter six pence a window, which led to many being bricked up, and encouraged the construction of the elongated top storey weaving windows still to be seen in many silk and cotton towns.

Religious records, deeds and documents, as well as private papers and valuables were stored in the solid church chest. It was purposely fitted with three different locks. The priest and the two churchwardens each kept a key so that all three had to be present whenever it was opened to prevent any pilfering. Parish armour and bows and arrows were often stored in the Parvis, the room above the porch, where the priest had lived in former times. The churchwardens had to inspect everything twice a year to make sure it was serviceable in case of invasion. On Sundays, all male members had to practice archery for two hours after divine service, or pay a penalty of tuppence. That is why so many fields near to churches are called 'the butts' - where the round straw targets were erected.

During the 1600s the emphasis of worship gradually moved from the altar to the pulpit. People became restless, standing for up to three hours at a time. Slowly a little more comfort was introduced into churches. Earthen floors were flagged or boarded and seats installed called pews. Faculties allowed the freehold purchase of pews and owners kept them under lock and key. The wardens collected high fees from the largest pews at the front and less for those at the back. Paupers were crammed 'freely' onto wooden benches at the rear, or sat huddled in corners.

The wardens had to stoke and enliven the central fire during the singing of the hymn before the sermon, so that hopefully the singing drowned out the noise. Servants also took victuals to the rich to sustain them through the long and often boring

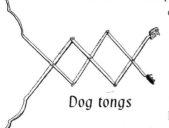

Dog tongs

sermon. But the combination of full stomachs, warmth and comfort posed yet another problem. It was the wardens' duty to keep the congregation awake during the sermon. To help them they had a whip, which would be 'cracked' over the head of any unfortunate male slumberer. Ladies got off more lightly, for at the other end of the whip handle was a feather - to tickle her under her nose - which not only aroused her but frequently made her sneeze, much to the amusement of all around. The whip was also used to drive stray or disobedient dogs out of church, if dog tongs were not to hand.

Illegitimate children caused many a headache for the hard-pressed wardens, especially after the 1750s. Any child so entered into the baptismal register became a settled citizen and was entitled to relief from the church coffers of a shilling per week and half a loaf of bread. At the age of seven the child was considered old enough to fend for itself and earn its own keep. By the early 1800s the problem had grown, the church found it was funding about one child in every eight. The cost had risen to two shillings per child per week, and it played havoc with the cash in the kitty - which is where the wardens stepped in. They were local people who knew the most likely father. They hauled him before the magistrates who imposed a charge of fifty pounds on him to cover the cost of rearing the child.

If the real father couldn't be found, one was 'provided' from the young men of the parish. Few prospective fathers could afford to pay, so they were placed in the 'clink' until the formalities had been completed and the banns read. On their wedding day the 'father' was escorted into church to marry the mother, flanked on either side by the churchwardens carrying their staves of office ('knobsticks') to make sure he did not escape the ceremony. From then onwards those weddings of convenience for the church, and often inconvenience for the couple, were termed 'knobstick weddings!'

The churchwardens must have heaved a sigh of relief at the church ales on the Tuesday after Easter, when they were invited to a free dinner by the 'Vestry' to celebrate the end of their year's stewardship. There they could relax and smoke - another symbol associated with their dignified office - their long stemmed 'churchwarden' pipes.

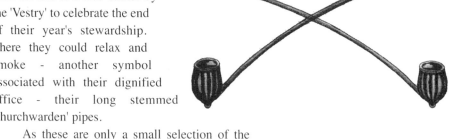

As these are only a small selection of the multitude of duties that churchwardens were expected to perform in the past, it's little wonder that many preferred to pay the heavy fine, rather than tackle the onerous task. Why, in comparison, there's nothing to the job nowadays, is there?!!

49 May Ley Lines
UNSOLVED MYSTERIES OF THE MAN-MADE MOUNDS

Did you know that many of our cathedrals, churches and crosses are built on a foundation of former religions, or that there is a direct link between the landmarks of yesteryear (barrows, tumuli and standing stones) and the Rogation-tide customs and Ascension Day processions of today? It is intriguing, but true! Scattered, seemingly at random, across the countryside of Europe and the Middle East are man-made mounds and standing stones that were erected by our Neolithic ancestors up to six thousand years ago. They emphasised the points at which fluctuating energy flowed from the surface of the earth and could be utilised - and possibly harnessed.

The strange fact about them is that when they are plotted on a map or traced on the ground, they uncannily connect into a series of straight lines, which vary in length from a short distance to hundreds of miles! Even more puzzling is that a few of the lines indicate the position of sunrise on 1st May or 1st November. Some show sunrise and sunset at the midsummer or midwinter solstice. Others act as star calendars, but the meaning behind the majority remains a mystery.

With the passing of time, some of these lines became the trackways of traders in salt, precious stones, minerals and metals. Others led pilgrims along their paths to sacred shrines. The Romans paved sections and turned them into straight roads. Cattle drovers used them as green lanes and recently the ridge-ways have become the haunt of ramblers.

Changes have also taken place on the mounds - the barrows and tumuli. Because these sites periodically exuded feelings of energy and euphoria, it was on and around them that people originally congregated to worship their Gods, hold feasts and festivals, and to barter and trade. It is well known that each new cult used the devotional places of its predecessors as a base for its own religion. So it was, that the conquering Celts utilised these mounds and from them their high priests, the Druids, invoked the power of their Gods which we still perpetuate with the names of the days of our week. The invading Romans used the same sites to build temples to their Gods. Then came the early Christian missionaries. They purified the Roman temples and consecrated them into the first Christian churches. Over nine thousand abbeys, priories, monasteries, cathedrals and churches were built, largely on those sites, before 1500 AD.

When religious buildings went out of fashion, the nobility put their halls on them instead, and later often erected follies on others. Hill-top mounds were well positioned to act as camps, castles or fortifications.

Standing stones have an equally chequered history. The Greeks dedicated them to Hermes and they marked the position where two or more lines crossed - later crossroads. To move such a marking stone was a crime punishable by death. The Romans surmounted theirs with the bust of Mercury and used them as signposts, pointing out the direction of the lines - the roads! Other stones marked the boundaries and were called termini. It was an offence to disfigure or remove them. In this country traders from the different directions gathered at the crossroads, the mark or merc (mercury) stones, to buy and sell their animals and produce. This is why the area came to be called a market and why the traders were known as merchants.

When Christianity arrived it surmounted the stone with a cross, so it became the Market Cross, and if it was damaged, 'Broken Cross'! As parishes started to develop, some of the outlying 'mark' stones marked the boundaries and became 'landmarks'. When the church took control of the parish, the villagers had to process around the boundary every year to make sure that no marker had been moved out of line. To impress upon the younger members the exact position of each mark site, they were beaten on the bottom with willow wands. Hence the custom that the church continues on Ascension Day - 'beating the bounds'.

Sometimes the standing stones were incorporated in the building of the church, either as the altar stone or as part of the walls - the foundation stone - having their source of energy spiralling underneath. This started the tradition of laying a special stone to symbolise the whole of the foundations; with votive gifts buried underneath to appease the Gods, who would stop subsidence, collapse or any other disaster striking it. In the 1550s the use of stone altars was forbidden, since some of them had been used for pre-Christian sacrifice. Many were destroyed and replaced by wooden Mensas or Communion Tables'.

Living on some of these ancient sacred sites were wise sages called hermits - the followers of Hermes, the Greek messenger of the Gods. The Roman equivalent was Mercury! The hermit's task was to guide travellers along the straight lines through the forests and swamps, to ferry or ford them across rivers, and lead them to the next hermit, or he pointed out further 'landmarks' for the traveller to aim at. If a hermit served a site for a sufficient number of years the area was called a castle. This may help to explain why so many places bear the name but have no fortifications on them.

Pious people who lived in a tiny cell without a door were called anchorites (from the Egyptian, Ankr). They stayed entombed, their provisions were passed through a small window. Sometimes they had a fireplace. Their opinions were widely sought after. Within the walls of 'All Saints', the parish church of Macclesfield - now 'St Michael's' - lived John Prior, an anchorite who in 1509, for his piety, devotion and zeal, was given a grant by the Bishop of Lichfield.

Sacred sites that are higher than the surrounding landscape are frequently associated with stories of dragons. That was because of the name our ancestors gave to the pulsating energy that emanated from these sites - Dragon's Breath! Churches built on these prominent positions are usually dedicated to St. Michael, St. Margaret or St George, all of whom have close connections with dragons. The energy exuded (dragon's breath, orgone, etheric, it has many names) fluctuates according to the phases of the moon and the seasons.

Spiralling energies, often associated with blind springs, change direction six days after the new moon and again six days after the full moon. Forty days after the Spring and Autumn Equinox are 'high' periods - 1st May and 1st November, the ancient dates for the beginning of summer and winter. That is why our ancestors erected their maypole on the barrow or tumuli and danced around it or danced in and out of the circle of stones or between the pine trees. They were absorbing the earth's energies, then redirecting them onto the surrounding countryside, to ensure the future fertility of the fields - echoes of Rogationtide?

You don't believe a word of it? Then take an Ordnance Survey map, a plastic ruler and try lining up a few points that I've mentioned - barrows, tumuli, standing stones, churches, halls, straight tracks, crossroads, crosses, markets, shrines, abbeys, priories, cathedrals, camps, castles, forts, follies, ferries and fords - The results may surprise you.

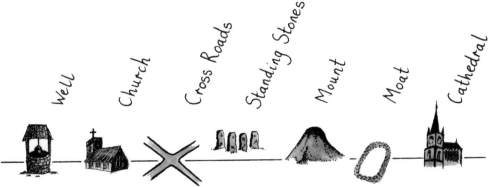

By the way, this theory was only discovered sixty years ago, by a corn merchant who travelled a great deal! Alfred Watkins was interested in why ancient places so frequently occurred along straight lines. He called them 'ley lines' because so many passed through places with Ley in the name. Alderley - the tumulus to the south of the Edge - has four leys passing through it. Chester Cathedral has six. Not convinced? Then try it for yourself - and good hunting.

50 June Sheep Shearing
HOW THE SHEEP CATCHER CAME A CROPPER

A sheep's fleece is its woollen overcoat, and just as we wouldn't dream of discarding our warm clothing whilst there was a nip in the air, shepherds were warned not to be impatient and shear their sheep too soon. "Shear your sheep in May and you'll shear them all away" was the old maxim, for centuries of experience had proved that ewes, chilled by cold conditions not only suffered themselves after the removal of their fleece, but also, because their milk-flow was disrupted, it caused a serious setback to their lambs. "Wait until a waxing moon, when the dog-rose is in full bloom" advised one saying. Another recommended "Do not start to shear sheep until the elderflowers begin to peep."

These ancient lores were rigorously observed for the well-being of the flock and the sheep-shearing season was, and still is traditionally, from the middle of June to the end of July. But preparations had to be put into practice well in advance. About two weeks before shearing, the fleeces were washed. On my previous farm this was done by damming a brook to raise the level of water. The sheep were then driven in and along it until their wool was thoroughly water-logged. A calm, warm day was always chosen for this job because if the sheep were too hot, they might have a heart attack when plunged into the cool river water. As the fleeces gradually dried the half inch growth of new wool next to the skin frizzed out. This meant that a neater, easier, cleaner and closer cut could be obtained, which would also yield a greater weight of wool than from unwashed sheep. It was considered well worth the extra effort.

Dipping crook

Antiquated but adequate clipping machine

Our sheep were shorn by a retired shepherd from Harper Adams Agricultural College. A tarpaulin sheet was laid on the yard to prevent any dirt getting on to the cleaned fleeces. My job was to catch the sheep for him and my wife and I took it in turns to turn the handle that powered his antiquated but adequate clipping machine. The shorn fleece was laid out flat, clipped side uppermost. The edges were folded inwards and the fleece rolled into a bundle. It was tied by twisting the neck wool into a rope band, which was firmly bound around the folded fleece.

Binder twine or synthetic string must never be used to fasten the fleece, since some of the strands might get entangled in the wool. They had to be removed by hand when the clip was graded at the wool warehouse and resulted in a lower price being paid, as did dirty fleeces, any stained with tar, non-removable marking fluid, or those entwined with thorns, briars, sticky burrs or straw. So will be seen the sense of keeping everywhere and everything clean, before, during, and after clipping.

The shorn sheep were loosed into the paddock to a chorus of bleating as the little lambs tried to discover which was their mother as she emerged totally transformed in her new short-cropped summer outfit.

Before the advent of machine clippers, the wool was removed by sprung hand shears or large scissors, an arduous task, which fell at a very busy time of the year. It coincided with the hoeing of the root crops and also haysel - haymaking. To try to overcome this disadvantage, family farmers on the mountains and moorlands often organised themselves into groups. They helped to shear one another's flocks. Each man's entitlement

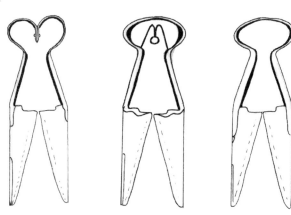

Three different types of sprung sheep shears

was to give one full day's work for every forty sheep that he had of his own to be shorn.

But the marshes and lowlands carried much larger flocks. Here the shearing was done by 'outside' gangs of odd-job men organised with the skill of a military operation. They would gather in the local pub on a Sunday evening to meet the shepherds from the surrounding farms, all attired in their best smocks. In charge of the gang was a 'captain' and his 'lieutenant', often ceremoniously dressed in white duck drill, adorned with gold braid and a blue tri-cornered hat. During the discourse a day suitable for each shepherd was allocated and 'drunk to' by all concerned. This arrangement enabled the shepherd to keep his sheep under cover the night beforehand, for cold sheep with rain or dew-drenched fleeces held their wool tightly to the skin, were difficult to shear and an unsightly stubble was left. But the wool on warm sheep, wearing dry fleeces, came up 'frizzed out'. They could be cut quicker and looked smarter when finished, which was to everyone's advantage.

The captain, lieutenant and their gang - this time in their working clothes - started between 5 and 6am. On arrival at the farm they first erected a clean shearing platform, utilising the large barn doors, levelled on brick pillars, working outside if dry and inside the barn if wet. Each shearer was expected to fleece one ewe every twenty minutes; three sheep to the hour, then he could have a short break and a horn of beer. After another two sheep he would 'pull up and sharpen' - straighten up his back, whetstone his shears and have another horn beaker of beer - with a touch of gin in it. Quick snacks were also provided, tiffin, bagin and beaver. Dewbit at 7 am, breakfast at 9 am, then elevenses, a longer break for dinner at 1 o'clock, followed by 'fourses', then tea at 6 o'clock. They aimed to finish by 8pm and clean themselves up ready for a slap-up meal and merrymaking provided by the farmer and his staff at 9 o'clock. The men would wash themselves in buckets of soft water containing sprigs of wild flowering mint. This effectively removed the greasy lanolin and replaced some of the smell of sheep with mint.

In 1900 they received five shillings (25p) per score (twenty sheep) and so earned ten shillings per day (50p). This was as much as the farm labourer was paid for a week, but it was hard graft, sore wrists for several days and an ever aching back! Slipped discs and hernias were an occupational hazard for the older men, especially when catching the sheep, so younger men were usually relegated to that task.

As I discovered from experience, the first few sheep were easily caught in the tightly packed fold, but. as the evening wore on there were fewer sheep and more room for the remainder to manoeuvre. Meanwhile the conditions underfoot became more and more slippery. Eventually the inevitable happened, trying to catch one of our timid Welsh hill ewes my feet slipped and I fell headlong into it - to the cheers and chuckles of the onlookers. I'd been initiated - if that's the right word!

Farmers have always maintained that the lamb and wool crops were just as important a harvest as the root and corn crops. So, when all the sheep were shorn, the farmer would invite everyone who had helped to a special 'shearing feast' of food, fun and frolics. But it was the shepherd, if he was still sober at the end of the festivities, who was called upon to give the final toast:

> If I had store
> By sheep and fold,
> I'd give you gold;
> But, since I'm poor,
> By crook and bell,
> I wish you well.

51 July Take it With a Pinch of Salt
DELICACY SOUGHT BY CATTLE AND CANNIBALS ALIKE

Many missionaries have lost their lives because they had it in their blood. Roman soldiers were paid a part of their wages with it. Social classes were formerly divided by it. Witches, demons and evil spirits were kept at bay with it. Errant sailors dreaded it. Animals love to lick it. For centuries it has been one of Cheshire's most important industries, obtained from the three 'wych' towns of Northwich, Middlewich and Nantwich. I expect by now you will have guessed from the clues that it is the condiment you add with the vinegar to your chips. It is the ingredient that remains unnoticed until mum forgets to use it when cooking the vegetables: Essential to all of us - SALT.

It circulates round our bodies in the bloodstream and, when we sweat, a small amount of it exudes through the pores of our skin, which is why animals like to lick us; it helps them to make up any deficiency in their diet. In hot weather people require extra salt to avoid dehydration. Primitive tribesmen, in tropical countries far from the sea and deprived of salt, discovered this fact and consequently some became cannibals! It was, therefore, a heaven sent opportunity to obtain an additional supply by making a meal of a meandering missionary! I often wonder if that has any connection with the Arabic custom of hospitality when you eat salt with your host as a gesture of friendship?

Even in ancient times salt was highly valued as the symbol of purity. It was used in sacrifices by the Greeks, Romans and Jews. Genesis explains how Lot's wife was turned into a pillar of salt when she defied God's command and looked back to see the destruction of the cities of Sodom and Gomorrah whilst escaping with her husband and daughters.

A covenant of salt (Numbers 18 v19) was a promise that must never be broken. In the New Testament Jesus told his disciples that they were the salt of the earth - the best - the elite. But if salt has lost its savour wherewith shall it be salted? If men had fallen from grace how could they be restored? Here Jesus alluded to the fact that if rock salt is left out in the hot sun it will lose its saltiness. Over the centuries salt became sacred and associated with God. To spill the salt was to break the bond. Fortunately the wrath of God, evil omen or quarrel might be averted if a pinch was thrown three times (Father, Son and Holy Ghost) over the LEFT shoulder into the face of the devil with the right hand (God's hand). In the painting of 'The Last Supper', Leonardo da Vinci identifies Judas Iscariot by the salt cellar which Judas has 'accidentally' just knocked over with his arm!

Salt was placed in the cradle to protect the child and in the coffin to protect the corpse against the influence of witches and evil spirits, because they were compelled to count every grain before they could cast a spell and so they never had time to complete their task! Similarly, glass tubes of salt were hidden in house walls over doors and windows. Salt was sprinkled on the doorsteps of new houses. Milkmaids put a pinch in the bottom of their buckets before milking, butter-makers in their churns and brewers on their mash to stop unwanted forces gaining access. But you must never put salt on anyone else's plate, for to help them to salt is to help them to sorrow.

At the end of each year divination was practised. A thimbleful of salt was piled upon each person's plate and left overnight. If anyone's mound had fallen by day-break, mourning would follow - they would die within the year. Salt carried into the house by the 'first foot' of the New year symbolised wealth. This originated from the salt rations (salary) that the Romans served out to their soldiers and civil servants in lieu of payment. When money was substituted this stipend went by the name 'salary' - from the Latin for salt.

In medieval times a massive silver salt cellar (saler) separated the upper and lower classes at mealtimes. The head of the household, his family and distinguished guests sat above the salt, the servants (villains) below. After a day's deer hunting only those who sat above the salt were allowed to eat the meat - venison. Those who sat below had to be content with the 'umbles' - heart, liver and entrails, baked in a crusty pie. As the pun says they had to eat 'humble pie'.

Before refrigeration fish and meat could be kept edible for long periods by encasing them in salt or soaking them in barrels of brine. In hot weather or on distant sea voyages the meat might still turn rancid. But the meal that sailors dreaded above all others was 'the taste of salt eel for supper'. This was the name given to punishment by flogging with the nine eelskin thongs of the 'cat o'nine tails'. It was administered on deck if the weather was fine, or in their cramped quarters below decks if foul - where there wasn't enough room to swing the 'cat'! To add insult to injury, salt was rubbed into the wounds, making them smart even more. But, acting as a counter-irritant, it reduced the risk of infection, brought blood to the area and helped the healing. Sleeping in a hammock was certainly not very comfortable afterwards!

Cat o' nine tails

It is said that even the most improbable stories can be swallowed with a pinch of salt, in other words if they contain a grain of truth. When I was young and couldn't catch my pet hen or rabbit, my uncle used to chide me and say 'put a bit of salt on its tail, boy'. And 'Smiths' never made much impact in the potato crisp market until a salesman decided to include a portion of salt in a blue paper wrapper - then sales rocketed!

In Cheshire the brine wells used to be dressed in flowers and blessed with thanksgivings on Ascension Day. Half a ton of fuel was needed to boil each ton of salt in small pottery or leaden dishes two feet square and three inches deep. Each held about seven gallons of brine, which boiled down to fourteen pounds of salt. It took about sixteen boilings to fill the wicker panniers of each packhorse. Trains of hardy 'fifteen-hand' Galloway packhorses tied tail to halter in strings of twenty or more each carried their two hundredweight loads through our villages. The 'whiteman' in charge brought up the rear. One mischievous pony found that if he lay in the river when crossing the ford his salt would dissolve and his burden was lighter. But the experienced tail driver soon cured him, for on his next journey the panniers contained rags instead. They absorbed the water and the pony then had twice as much weight to carry!

Places on route were named after the product, Sale, Salford, Saltersford and, locally, Salters Lane and Salt Hall. There were also the salt pits where illicit cargo could be hurriedly dumped when chased by customs officials if the heavy excise duty had not been paid. A field nearby is called 'Gallows Rise', suggesting a rough and ready retribution for anyone unlucky enough to be caught.

Until fairly recently salesmen would call at my farm with large irregular lumps of brown streaked rock salt for sale. Every cow had some in her stall and every calf in its manger. New methods of production have changed the old ideas and I am now offered a choice of red, white or blue salt licks for my stock. Each block is of a precise cubic shape with a hole in the middle, which I use for suspending it on a baler twine rope from a lower branch of the oak tree near the cross-roads. My cattle love them and they lick away until the corners converge and four more holes appear in the diagonals, making the block look like a gigantic super 'Polo' mint.

Yes, it certainly does take a bit of licking - does SALT.

52 August Rabbits, Rabbits, Rabbits
**A RABBIT BOOM SOUNDS THE
ALARM FOR FARMERS**

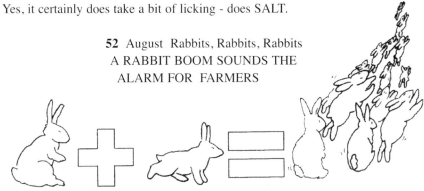

Apart from the continuing cold wet weather the main talking point amongst farmers and countrymen this summer has been the alarming increase in the number of rabbits. "They're back again, droves of them," says one. "Yes, we're over-run with them, as bad as before the myxy (myxomatosis) twenty years ago," says another. "They're that thick on the ground, they have to queue up to get down their burrows," a third chips in, "I heard they caught over a hundred in one night's shooting and got sixty from the same field the next night."

According to your taste, rabbits are either adored, encouraged, tolerated or destroyed. They are generally adored by the very young, the very old and readers of books such as 'Watership Down'. Encouraged if you are a shooting or sporting enthusiast. Tolerated, as part of the country scene by the majority of us - providing they don't cause us any inconvenience; or destroyed to the point of annihilation by nurserymen, arable farmers and foresters, who have a lot to lose from their presence, and therefore have a vested interest in their destruction.

Rabbits haven't always been with us. Nobility introduced them from Europe in the 12th Century to provide sport, fur and help eke out their winter rations of fresh meat. Warreners were employed to breed 'conies' in special fenced enclosures called 'greaves' as is recorded for posterity by the name of one of the fields on my farm - 'Coneygreave', the rabbit warren. Inevitably some escaped and set up colonies of their own.

It was only two hundred years ago that they became such a pest, and an Act of Parliament allowed landowners to destroy rabbits to protect their crops. But their control seems to have passed to the low paid farmworkers who regarded the rabbit as an additional perk and which, until recently, helped to fill his stockpot. As well as relying on wild rabbits, William Cobbett wrote in his book 'Cottage Economy' in 1820, that three domesticated does and a buck would provide a family with a meal of rabbit meat every third day throughout the year, at practically no cost. Certainly in my younger days every country cottage had its cluster of cages by the back door. They contained Flemish Giants, Belgian Hare, Lop-Ears or the attractive Black and White or Blue and White Dutch Rabbits that were the children's pets, and of course some cuddly Angoras for their fluffy white wool.

Almost any convenient container served as a hutch. Wooden egg boxes, orange boxes, twelve gross match boxes or tea chests - in which the plywood went crinkly when they got wet! They had a corrugated tin or felt roof to keep out the worst of the weather and a wire netting door for light and air. Highly sought after were discarded beer barrels. When laid on their sides they were warm and weather and draught-proof. With a few holes bored underneath to allow any effluent to escape, and bedded with sweet smelling hay or straw they made cosy homes for breeding does.

In spring, summer and autumn the tame rabbits were fed twice a day with surplus greenstuff from the garden. This was supplemented with fresh dandelions, hog-weed, elm leaves, twigs and branches and almost anything green gathered free from the hedge banks by the children coming home from school or father from his work. Sheep's parsley was included only by those who knew the difference between its triangular leaf stem and the similar looking but deadly poisonous round stemmed hemlock! In winter food was never given if frozen, it would make them scour and lose condition. Potato peelings, carrot tops, swedes, beet, kale and cabbage leaves, fresh hay and, if affordable, a few oats completed their winter diet.

When mature they were killed instantaneously by a 'rabbit punch' - a sharp blow to the back of the neck with the edge of the hand. Home fed rabbits had several advantages over their wild counterparts. There were no broken bones, the meat was tender, not bruised and it contained no lead shot. Rabbit skins were valuable - when dried the fur was sold to make felt for the hat trade. When cured, the skins made children's toys, clothes ('Bye baby bunting'), gloves and fur socks to prevent pleurisy and other kindred ills. The front right foot was kept for good luck or sold to apply make-up to the faces of gentlewomen or those on the stage. The tail (scut) with its white warning underside, when tied to a piece of string, improvised as a mouse to teach kittens to catch

vermin. And the nitrogen rich manure helped to swell the cottager's compost heap.

But the hard, black droppings from wild rabbits is not such a good fertiliser, for whenever feeding is sparse or grazing time is short due to predators or bad weather, the rabbit passes soft pellets and re-eats them. Passing through the system twice, it extracts more nutrients from less food - that's adaptability for you!

Their warrens contain all age groups in a peck order of social importance. In charge is the main buck, followed by former main bucks. Dominant does who nest deep in the warrens come next and, last of all, the young bucks and does. Periodically, the main buck will drive some of the young bucks away to colonise new warrens. Younger does nest in shallow stop holes in the field away from the warrens. This helps to prevent predators or bucks finding and killing the youngsters.

Rabbit's scut (tail)

The main breeding season is from November to July and the doe mates within two days of giving birth to an average of five 'kittens', as the young are called. Pregnancy lasts twenty-eight days and most does have at least four litters a season, some six. The young **have** to be weaned at four weeks, for that is when the next batch arrives! It is no wonder they say 'breed like rabbits!'

Before the rabbit flea transmitted the deadly myxomatosis virus to ninety-nine per cent of its host in 1954, there were two rabbits to every person in the country! Since then we have been able to grow bumper crops of corn, sugar beet and grass. Our fields are stocked so heavily that food is in surplus and we are stockpiling it. Who knows, if the rabbits keep increasing in numbers and nibbling away at our surpluses, we may soon be back to an era of shortages. Then we shall all have to live on rabbit pie every third day throughout the year!

53 September Corn Dollies
WHEN STRANGERS LOST THEIR HEADS OVER CORN GODDESS

What a summer we have had - if you can call it that. When it started I thought - this wet weather won't last, next month is bound to be better - but it wasn't it's got worse as it's gone on! This is the first time in over thirty years of farming that I have lost a field of hay. The daily showers and moisture-laden winds have meant that, even with the benefit of hindsight, at no time in the last five weeks could I have successfully harvested that particular field. It lies there, still rotting in the swath, a complete write-off, untouched since the day it was cut.

Yet, in spite of the exasperating conditions, I have more hay in the barn than for many years. Luckily I managed to snatch a batch during every short, fine spell that we had, and am much more fortunate than some of my compatriots, especially those on the hills. The cereal crops, too, have taken a battering. The laid corn, flattened by wind and rain, resolutely refuses to dry enough to allow the combine harvesters to gather the grain. To add to the difficulties, the constant dampness has encouraged some of the ears to grow. So, even when it is harvested, the sprouted grain will have to be artificially dried before it can be put into store - a very expensive operation. Corn seeds, like ourselves, only live once, and grains that have germinated this year will not grow again. They will have to be sold for animal feed, yielding a reduced income for the farmer. But with our modern methods of storage and our extensive surpluses carried over from previous years, one wet harvest no longer constitutes a calamity.

Barley

Oats

In the past such a failure foretold famine and misfortune in many a household. Corn stacked when wet went mouldy and caused chest complaints. Musty or germinated grain ground into a flour that remained bitty and lumpy and when baked boiled over, turned black and stuck to the tins or the oven floor. Families had to survive on charcoal scrapings instead of bread. So important was the corn harvest that all kinds of traditions and superstitions were rigidly observed to reduce the risk of failure.

Many of the origins have been traced back nine thousand years to the Middle East when our nomadic meat-eating ancestors started to settle down. The menfolk still spent much of their time hunting animals but the women began to grow wheat on the good ground and barley, oats and rye on the poorer soil. Some four thousand years later primitive ploughs were invented and domesticated animals were used to pull them. From then on men started to take a wider interest in the cultivation of the corn crops. They worshipped a mother figure, a goddess of the corn, associated with the mystery of germination, the fertility of man and beast, and the rituals connected with the living and the dead.

In Egypt she was called Isis, in Greece Demeter, whilst the Romans called her Ceres, from which we derive our word 'cereal'. She was thought to live in every field in spirit form. At harvest when the corn was being cut she would retreat into the last standing ears. In order to preserve her presence the reapers would fashion the last sheaf of straw into an effigy - an idol, or later a geometrical shape, into which the corn spirit would take refuge. She was carried aloft in a happy procession, home to the farmstead, where she was placed in a position of honour for the duration of the winter, protected from pests and predators, wind and weather. In the springtime another joyful procession carried the corn idol out into the freshly cultivated fields, where her 'cage' was broken open to liberate her impounded spirit, allowing it to roam freely to fertilise the newly sown grain and teach it how to grow.

If the seed failed to germinate, the explanation was simple. The reapers had failed to capture the corn spirit the previous harvest - she had escaped. Perhaps someone had left the gate open - or she had been carried off by a passing traveller. To prevent such a disaster happening, any luckless pilgrim or stranger passing at the end of harvest was bound up in the last sheaf and beheaded! A custom which may well have been perpetuated in Devon, by the end of harvest ceremony called 'Crying the Neck'

Both solid and hollow plaited straw shapes are now known as 'Corn Dollies'. Many people think that they should all have faces, arms and legs, but the word 'Doll' is simply a corruption of the old word 'idol'. So what some children take to bed with them at night are in fact their 'idols'! Corn Dollies were believed to contain the power to ward off witches and evil spirits. Solid straw finials in the shape of foxes, pheasants, cockerels and crosses were placed along the ridge of thatched roofs to stop broomstick-riding witches from landing. Whilst woven spiral plaits were hung at the eaves to prevent evil spirits from entering and spoiling sheaves that were stored out of doors in stacks. Each corn-growing area developed its own individual pattern of straw shapes. Kent had its Ivy Maid, which originated from Roman times, Norfolk its lantern, Suffolk's symbol was the horse-shoe, reminding us of the Suffolk Punch and the Newmarket races. Northumberland made a figure representing Mother Earth similar to the Scottish Clyack. This often held a 'kern' baby in its arms or had one hidden inside it. Plaited straw handbells from Cambridgeshire were replicas of those used to ring the last load of corn home from the fields.

9 straw plaited wheat

Young men made delicate lovers' knots called favours and presented them to the young lady of their choice. Acceptance meant that courting began in earnest. Other fine plaits, twisted into loops, were worn by those seeking work at hiring fairs. The number of circles gave your grade, and what it was made from, or tied with, your type of work - wool for a shepherd, leather for a carter and horsehair for a ploughman. Indeed they were the forerunners of today's buttonholes, badges and brooches that depict membership of a trade, religious belief or social club.

For over thirty-five years I have been teaching people to weave straws into intricate shapes. But what has amazed me most of all is the number of people who, having taken up this relaxing craft - or having received a corn dolly as a present - soon find that an addition to the family is on the way. So, before your fingers start itching to make a few corn dollies, and providing you can find some corn that hasn't been damaged by the atrocious weather we've had this summer, just remember - they are ancient symbols of fertility! But if you are still determined to have a go, I wish you the best of luck - and may they bring a little ray of sunshine into your life!

Spiral - the symbol of fertility

54 October Superstitions
BEWARE JENNY GREENTEETH AND THE EVIL SPRITES

Are you superstitious? Do you have any qualms about opening an umbrella indoors; consider it foolish to throw coins into a fountain; a waste of wine to break a bottle of champagne to launch a ship; or unhygienic to spit on your hands before starting a job? Although most people don't like to admit it, superstitions still play an important part in our lives. They resulted from a universal fear of the Gods, the unknown, the unpredictable and the unforeseen.

Superstitions became a safeguard, a ritual of rules and regulations that were rigorously enforced on every occasion to appease the wrath of the Gods and woe betide anyone who disobeyed or forgot to put them into practice. Some superstitions were based on common sense, such as not playing near wells or rivers, else 'Jenny Greenteeth' might reach out and pull you in. Others reminded us of the help that we can call upon in times of boastfulness, trouble or doubt. A rash statement is often followed by the phrase 'touch wood'. If no wood is within reach touch one's own head instead - in mockery! The origin was always to be on the right side of the tree spirits and pay homage by touching them in respect, rather as in olden days a servant touched his forelock when the squire passed by.

In later Christian times, it invoked the power of Christ, since the cross was made of wood. This is also the reason for crossing your fingers if in trouble and why religious people make the sign of the cross when embarking on a voyage in a ship or aeroplane - or they carry a talisman, a St Christopher medallion - the patron saint of travellers!

Another group of superstitions have passed through two or more phases before arriving at what we know and do today. Let me explain in a little more detail. You may be surprised to learn that the umbrella, because of its shape, is really associated with the sun! In the East, royalty and the highly privileged sat under a sun shade, a para-sol, to ward off the sun! The Sun God would be seriously offended if it was unnecessarily opened in the shade or in the house. Towards the end of the 17th Century, the wearing of swords by English gentlemen was gradually replaced by the carrying of an umbrella. With the change of fashion arrived the superstitions previously attached to the sun-shade - that it is unlucky to open it indoors. But beware - to open an umbrella outside in fine weather may also bring on the rain, and we've already had enough of that this summer.

Rivers and wells were thought to contain water sprites who periodically demanded a life. To placate them an expendable human sacrifice was offered instead. Over the years this changed to an animal sacrifice, then sacred stones or baked clay vessels were dropped into the waters as votive offerings. These also foretold your future. If the water bubbled and gurgled, the omens were favourable. If the water became cloudy, misfortune would follow. Bent pins were cast into the water to obtain good luck and, in modern mercenary times, money in the form of coins. You leaned over in homage, paid a tribute and wished - hence the 'wishing well'. In gratefulness for a continuous supply of well water in times of drought, the sprites were rewarded with garlands of flowers. Christianity deplored this practice and set up its own alternative. 'Sian' the water sprites well (Ann in Ireland) became St. Anne's well; Brigid became St. Brigid's Well or Brideswell and religious ceremonies were held each Rogationtide. In 1818 the first floral decorations of petals pressed into patterns to form pictures on a base of dampened clay started what we now call 'Well Dressings'.

The origin of breaking

a bottle of champagne over a ship's bow when launching is even more complex. The male Sea Gods, Neptune and Poseidon, claimed the soul of the first to die on any vessel. To counteract this a female was sacrificed over the prow as it entered the water, so that all future souls could pass to paradise. In course of time the human sacrifice was replaced by an animal, but the female figure was still often represented by a figure head. With the advent of Christianity the sacrificial blood was replaced by red wine (in a parallel manner to the communion wine). From red wine it changed to the best wine obtainable - champagne. But the name of the ship remains proudly painted on the bow to remind us in part of the gruesome origins of what is now taken for granted.

A similar superstition once existed on dry land, when people believed that the devil claimed the soul of the first internment in a newly consecrated graveyard. To confound him a black cat, black dog or goat was usually buried first. One superstition that has changed and by doing so has become incorrect, is that a rabbit's foot is lucky - it isn't. Originally it was the hare whose foot was lucky, because baby hares (leverets) are born with their eyes open, and can 'see off' evil. When Christianity changed the custom to rabbits, it was conveniently forgotten that baby rabbits are born blind!

If a youngster falls down and is hurt, someone will say 'let me kiss it better'. The child's attention is diverted, the pain disappears and no more tears. It dates back to the days when poison was sucked from wounds to lessen the dangers of infection. Spittle, like blood, was once thought to be the centre of soul power and the first spittle of the morning was applied to wounds to heal them; and to warts, birthmarks, swellings and ringworm to remove them. You spat to avoid contact with evil on seeing a magpie, a piebald horse or a

cross-eyed person. It was good luck for a trader to spit on the
first money received in the day. It would encourage more, as it
did to the traveller's money on first sighting the new moon. The
'fastenpenny' at the hiring fair received the same treatment - it
sealed the bargain. If two people washed in the same water, a spit
would avoid a quarrel, and if you wished for extra strength in a
fight, or before starting work, you spat on your hands!

Babies were thought to be under the control of the fairies
until they sneezed. Idiots always were - if they couldn't sneeze! And
did you realise that when you sneezed it was a sign of the devil
coming out of you? This is one of the reasons why we say 'Bless you'
- before he can get back in! But he will get back in if you sleep with
your mouth open, or yawn without covering your mouth with your
hand. And, by the way, there is only one yawn, it's very catching, and it
continues around the world. You don't believe it? - then just yawn in company, and see
the effect it has on others. But don't start itching in company, because:

> If your left ear itches your lover is thinking of you
> Your right ear itches - it's your mother thinking of you.
> Your left eye itching - denotes a disappointment,
> But your right eye itching - a sign of a surprise.
> When our left palm itches - you will pay some money out,
> But if your right palm itches - you will have some money coming in.
> If your nose itches - you've got company coming
> And when your head itches - THEY'VE ARRIVED!

55 November Storage Clamps
VANISHED MOUNDS THAT KEPT JACK FROST AT BAY

No longer do you see them stretching along the entire length of the roadside headlands of
the harvested root fields, or protruding in haphazard heaps like giant molehills, on the
sheep folding turnip fields, awaiting the onset of winter. Not so very long ago, no
industrious cottager's garden would have been complete without at least one standing
sedately in it at this season of the year. What were they? - they were the frost-proof earth
covered storage clamps that protected the winter's rations of roots, potatoes,
mangelwurzels, swedes, turnips, carrots and parsnips. Even apples and dahlia tubers could
be safely stored at practically no cost, except a bit of warming work. Country people called
these clamps 'hogs' because when finished they looked like a hog's back.

In the early days of my farming career the harvesting of both potatoes and mangolds
was in full swing by the beginning of October. When the weather was too wet to lift
potatoes or if we hadn't sufficient pickers, we worked in the mangolds. Their large red or
yellow globes had to be pulled up, the leaves removed and four rows of growing roots put
into one row for convenience of carting. To defoliate them the leaves were grasped in the

left hand, the shallow rooted mangold lifted and swung towards the right hand. This held a very sharp 'fashing' hook, often fashioned from an old scythe blade. The hook stayed still, its keen knife edge severing the leaf stems as they passed. The momentum of the mangold propelled it into a precise position on the row of cut roots.

Fearful farmworkers or those whose hands were a bit shaky, screwed the leaves off instead! But it was rare to cut yourself with the knife. Mangolds are very susceptible to frost, so if it threatened they were either covered with their own leaves for protection or carted quickly. Once cut, they sweated for about a fortnight, after which they could be safely stacked to a considerable height indoors or clamped in the field.

Initially potatoes were lifted by forks. The man dug under the rows from the side, raising the round tubers to the surface. Then he, his wife, or children gathered the crop into shallow sieve-like oval baskets that allowed any adhering soil to fall through. When full, these were tipped into sacks or carts and carried to the clamp. Fork lifting was superseded by the ridging plough fitted with long metal fingers behind the shares. This in turn gave way to the potato spinner. Its share lifted the roots and its studded wheels drove rotating flails which flirted the crop sideways to the pickers. With the advent of tractors nearly all horse-drawn implements were adapted to mechanical motivation. Tractor wheels were so craftily designed that within a few minutes the width between them could be altered, allowing the tyres to tread in the spaces between the rows.

Having harvested the crop, the next step was to store it, safe from the keen frosts of winter. A dry, well drained and sheltered site was required. To save wasting time by carting it further afield, this was frequently the headland on which the crop was grown. The base of the future clamp was levelled to a width of about six feet. Cart loads of produce were backed along the line of the clamp and tipped. As the crop settled to its natural angle, any roots that rolled outside the required width were forked up to fill the gaps caused by irregular tipping. Special forks called scovens were used. These had knobs or a bar at the end of tines to prevent them puncturing the roots, for that would allow bacteria to enter and rot to set in.

Most clamps or hogs ended up triangular in shape, about four foot wide and four feet tall. Next, layers of straight straw (from battens, not bales) were laid vertically, covering the sides to a depth of about six inches, until the whole clamp was encased in a cocoon of straw thatch. Cottager's clamps often utilised thick layers of bracken, which was even cheaper! Spadefuls of soil were placed every foot or so to hold the covering in place in case of high winds. If the crop was immature or freshly harvested, the clamp remained strawed up for at least two weeks. This allowed the normal process of fermentation to heat the hog and expel any surplus moisture.

Only when the temperature inside had started to fall, was it safe to cover the straw with a six inch layer of earth, always remembering to leave some downward sloping tufts of straw at intervals along the top ridge to counteract changes in atmospheric pressure - or as they used to say - 'to let it breathe'.

Since the soil was dug from immediately around the edges, it formed a dry 'moat', with the clamp high and dry in the middle. To prevent the 'moat' filling during a prolonged spell of wet weather a drainage channel was dug onto lower ground or into an adjacent ditch. Additional insulation was given by covering the whole hog with hedge brushings - old grass, thorns, twigs and brambles that would otherwise have been burnt. They helped to keep Jack Frost at bay.

The clamp was inspected regularly to see that it was still secure. If potatoes or mangolds were touched by frost before clamping they might appear sound, but soon went rotten. The outward signs were cracks in the soil covering or even a complete collapse! The offending patch had to be ruthlessly cleared and the remaining area resealed or the trouble would quickly spread to adjacent sound roots.

When I was a lad we also clamped the crop from our orchard of four hundred trees of Bramley seedling apples on a bed of dry wheat straw. They kept juicy, sweet and fresh, until we could reap the reward of a higher price for them the following spring. The only trouble I can ever remember was one hard winter (1947?), when some rats tried to invade the clamp. Luckily they were spotted and caught before any damage was done.

Yes, we always made our 'hogs' at this time of year. So, whenever we get a spell of cold, damp, dreary days during November, I still get a glow of satisfaction when I think of how we used to keep warm - earthing up the storage clamps.

56 December Farmyard Design
FARMING 'PROGRESS' GOES BACK TO WHERE IT ALL BEGAN!

It was no accident that so many of our farmyards were built to a similar design after the beginning of the agricultural revolution in 1750. It came as the direct result of long tiring years spent in hard practical experience and observation. The most frequently found pattern was a large square yard, surrounded on three sides by double storeyed buildings. On the fourth - and usually the warmer southern side - stood the farmhouse, positioned so that the prevailing south westerly winds would blow many of the farmyard smells away from it.

About half way down the eastern side were the stables, specially sited so that in winter they would catch the first light of dawn and the last light of dusk. The doors were much wider than those built today because originally they housed not horses but horned ox-teams. Harness hung from wooden pegs plugged into the wall behind them. Oxen ate straw and were bedded on straw. Horses ate hay and stood on stone setts which had grooved spaces between them to allow their urine to flow away freely. This helped the horses to stand dry and avoid many of their foot complaints.

Next came the barn with a wagon-wide passageway in the middle and adjoining bays on either side. High double doors allowed the full loads of corn to enter; lower double doors on the opposite side allowed the empty wagons to leave - an ancient one way system! The sheaves of corn were stacked in the bays and, in winter, were threshed by hand flails or later by a horse driven thresher in the central passage.

Stretching the whole length of the north side stood open fronted, south facing covered yards. Here, loose housed bullocks (castrated bulls) and female heifers were fattened. As they milled around they mixed their dung with vast quantities of straw and turned it into ever deepening layers of valuable manure. Their long wooden feeding troughs were suspended on chains from the rafters. They could be lifted a few links, periodically to keep them above the rising level of manure.

Behind these yards and facing north were the cart sheds; where wagons, tumbrils, seed drills, harrows and other implements were stored. They were sheltered from the ravages of the rain that would otherwise warp the woodwork, rot the timbers and rust the ironwork. The north west corner contained a smaller storehouse where the animal feed was mixed. Swedes, turnips or mangolds (mangelwurzels) were carted in daily to be sliced into juicy finger lengths in the rotary cutters. Chaff, chopped straw or hay and meal were added and the resultant mixture was wheeled away in iron tyred wooden wheelbarrows or carried in wicker-work skeps. through the many doors and along the feeding passages (locally called 'bings') to the stock. Double quantities of food were prepared on Saturday to save work on Sundays.

Adjacent, on the west side, were the cows. They were tied to their wooden stall divisions by knotted rope halters, which passed through a round wooden ball called a 'chog' to allow for movement. In later years the rope was replaced by leather and then by neck chains. Running the length of the shed behind the cows was a wide channel or groupe

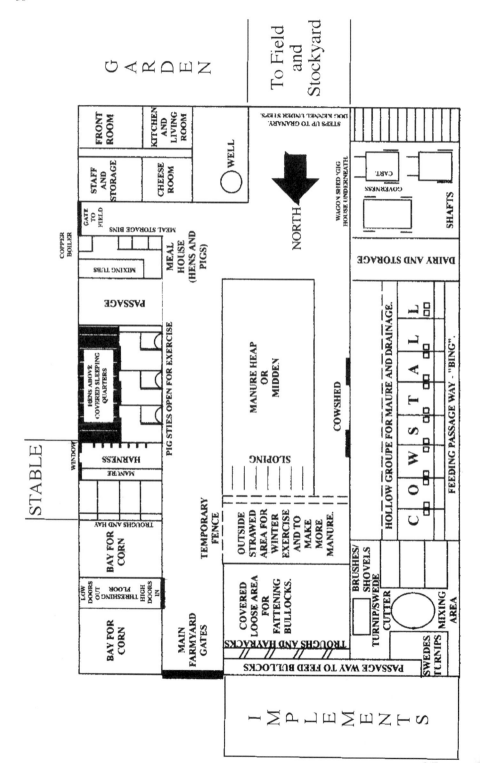

G A R D E N

To Field and Stockyard

NORTH

WELL

FRONT ROOM

KITCHEN AND LIVING ROOM

STAFF AND STORAGE

CHEESE ROOM

STEPS UP TO GRANARY. DOG KENNEL UNDER STEPS.

GATE TO FIELD

MEAL STORAGE BINS

MIXING TUBS

COPPER BOILER

MEAL HOUSE (HENS AND PIGS)

PASSAGE

WAGON SHED YGIG HOUSE UNDERNEATH

CART.

GOVERNESS.

DAIRY AND STORAGE

SHAFTS

HENS ABOVE COVERED SLEEPING QUARTERS

PIG STIES OPEN FOR EXERCISE

HARNESS

MANTRE

WINDOW

STABLE

TROUGHS AND HAY

BAY FOR CORN

LOW DOORS OUT

HIGH DOORS IN

THRESHING FLOOR

BAY FOR CORN

MAIN FARMYARD GATES

TEMPORARY FENCE

MANURE HEAP OR MIDDEN

SLOPING

OUTSIDE STRAWED AREA FOR WINTER EXERCISE AND TO MAKE MORE MANURE.

COVERED LOOSE AREA FOR FATTENING BULLOCKS.

TROUGHS AND HAYRACKS

PASSAGE WAY TO FEED BULLOCKS

COWSHED

HOLLOW GROUPE FOR MAURE AND DRAINAGE.

C O W S T A L L

FEEDING PASSAGE WAY - "BING".

BRUSHES/ SHOVELS

TURNIP/SWEDE CUTTER

MIXING AREA

SWEDES TURNIPS

I M P L E M E N T S

to contain the manure. Cowshed and stable doors were made in two parts. The upper half could be opened to give extra light and ventilation, whilst the lower half remained closed to stop floor draughts and prevent any loose stock escaping. Milk was cooled and the utensils cleaned in the adjoining dairy. Finally, on the west side, was the granary or garner, purposely built in the upper storey to keep it airy and the floor free from rising damp. Being high it also had the advantage that wagon loads of grain could be backed underneath and the hessian sacks hoisted up through trap-doors by block and tackle, all under cover - very handy in wet weather.

Because it was so near to the house, the farmer usually stored his trap, milk float and his wife's governess cart in the bays under the granary, often referred to as the Gighouse. The main approach to the granary was an outside flight of steep stone steps. At threshing times it was up these that all the grain was carried in $1^1/_2$ or even 2 cwt (hundredweight) sacks on the workmen's backs. You needed to be fit to keep that job up all day; I know, because I've had to do it many a time! In the hollow cavity under the steps was the dog kennel - to prevent pilferers stealing the grain at night. The granary door contained a cat hole and the apex of the gable end an owl hole to control other vermin.

Part of the farmhouse was often an extension of the dairy. The cooled milk was carried across and poured into vats to allow the cream to rise. This was skimmed off for making butter or curdled for cheese. Bucketfuls of skimmed milk, buttermilk and cheese drainings were mixed with meal and house scraps to fatten the pigs. Their sties stood between the house and the stables (on the eastern side). Above the pigs' sleeping quarters were hurdles for the hens to roost on at night. Free from the fear of foxes, the hens benefited from the rising warmth of the pigs - and the pigs benefited from the protein rich droppings of the hens!

Above the stables, fattening yards and cowsheds were fodder lofts. Each hay harvest these were filled through round pitching holes, a forkful at a time. The maturing hay was afforded adequate ventilation by the absence of individual bricks, often forming intricate diamond or cross shaped patterns on the side and end walls. Holes in the loft floors over the feeding racks and cratches meant that hay could be forked down easily whenever required - all under cover. This saved a lot of unpleasant outdoor work in bad weather. Any

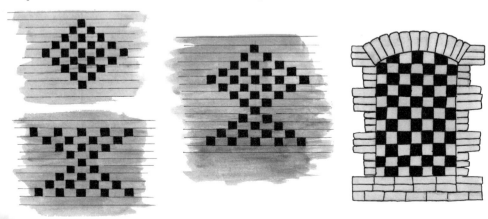

remaining free loft space was used to finish the fattening of cockerels and turkeys that had been reared on the stubbles and until then housed in their triangular movable night arks.

The large enclosed yard was an ideal sheltered exercise area for the cows in winter. In the middle stood the manure-heap, midden or mixen as it is also called - a central disposal site for all the manure barrowed from the pigsties, stables and cowsheds. With the manure from the fattening yards, it provided a sufficient supply of that vital ingredient so essential to maintain the future fertility of the fields, and the prosperity of the farm.

The advantages of this arrangement of buildings continued even after the working day was finished. For at night the farmer could still see and hear all that was happening around him - from the comfort of his own farmhouse.

Over the last thirty years another revolution has changed the farming scene. The old ideal of many small enterprises has been overtaken by the new idea of specialisation. Buildings have been gutted and massive milking parlours, pig, poultry or beef units installed. Fabricated, corrugated umbrella sheds have been erected. Silage clamps have replaced hay lofts. But the cycle of events is still revolving - during the last 12 months a 10 per cent cut back in milk production and a surplus of grain and potatoes have led many farmers to think about turning to other enterprises to try to maintain their income. Some are starting to re-utilise their redundant buildings and convert them into country workshops or self-catering units.

Who knows - if things continue moving forward, we may soon all be back where we began. That's progress for you! And a very happy.Christmas to you all.

57 January Cobblers - Worst Shod?
MYSTERY PARCELS STIRS MEMORIES OF THE PAST

There, standing almost as high as the Christmas tree, was the most unusual looking present I have ever seen. It had a large square base, surmounted by a stovepipe type of funnel, all covered in cardboard and swathed with sticky tape.

Whatever could it be?

My three-year-old grand-daughter, who had already put in quite a bit of practice unwrapping her own presents earlier that morning, helped me to remove the top. It concealed a tall wrought iron stem decorated with three twists and finishing with a scroll at the top.

I was still no wiser! We tore away at the bottom boxes until all was finally revealed..... two stiff yard brushes screwed - sideways on - to a sturdy four legged metal frame and joined by an upright bar underneath.

Have you guessed what it was? An old fashioned boot brush and scraper - made by my son-in-law. You don't see many of them about nowadays, do you? Flagged pavements, concreted paths and tarmacadamed roads have rendered these once essential objects almost obsolete - except for a few farmers and gardeners - who, like me, still come in with mud on their boots! Yet a few years ago no cottage scene would have been complete without its bootscraper by the back door and a long handled broom leaning against the wall to brush away the clinging clay. Even town tenements had a special recess built into the brickwork by the front door to accommodate the bootscraper. Nowadays these rounded holes are more likely to house the daily pintas and store the empties than to clean shoes.

But it isn't just the scrapers that have disappeared during the last few years. So too have the shoemakers and cobblers that were once such an important industry in every self supporting parish.

When Guilds of craftsmen were formed in the 1100s shoemakers were called Cordovanners or 'Cordwainers' because the goat-skins from which the best shoes were made at the time came from Cordova in Spain. Should the shoemaker tan his own leather using oak-bark, his surname might well become 'Barker'. And Northamptonshire, famous for its oak forests, also became famous for its footwear!

St. Crispin, himself a shoemaker, was their patron saint. His feast day (and also the date of the Battle of Agincourt) was October 25th, when shoemakers had a holiday. An ancient Suffolk quotation suggests that every Monday was a saint's day to shoemakers - they took the day off! They did a little on Tuesday, worked hard on Wednesday and Thursday and began to clear up on Friday and Saturday!

In order to obtain the correct shape the shoemaker first measured the feet. Then to allow for the thickness of the stocking a slightly oversize wooden copy was carved called a 'last'. Country people required a larger 'last' - for two pairs of woollen boot-hose or stockings in cold weather, or if they couldn't afford stockings an insulating layer of hay was used instead! Ill fitting boots, shoes or slippers gave rise to the saying 'slipshod'.

The shoemaker knew every one of his customers' requirements; each had his own 'last' and on them he fashioned their footwear in leather or fabric. To improve the waterproofing quality of his article they were often formed from one piece of material and only stitched at the top and rear. Holes were pierced with a sharp curved awl, called St. Crispin's Lance. In East Anglia it was given the nickname 'avocet' because of its similarity to that bird's beak. Strong hemp or flax threads were used for fastening. Each length was drawn over the 'heelball' - a mixture of beeswax and lampblack to stop it rotting - a pig's bristle was waxed on to one end to act as a needle. Two threads, worked in opposite directions, were used at the same time. When pulled tight they sealed the stitched seam.

Quarrels often broke out between 'Cordwainers' who were 'shoeMAKERS' and cobblers who were 'shoeMENDERS'. Cobblers were renowned for being lackadaisical. Like tinkers they travelled from place to place carrying their tools in a basket. When they found work they set up shop in the house if it was wet, or outside on the step if it was dry.

Foot measurer

They brought news from afar and gossip from just around the corner, sang the latest songs and whistled the latest tunes.

Later, quite an industry grew up when country cobblers - 'stitchmen' as they were called - began to make boots and shoes of standard sizes in their own homes or workshops.

One of the troubles with leather was that being thin it did not last very long, so many country people wore clogs - wooden soles of alder, birch or sycamore with leather uppers tacked on. The soles could have large headed 'hob' nails knocked into them and with metal strips protecting heels and toes they lasted much longer. Many a pensioner reading this may remember the Saturday mornings spent visiting the cobbler to have his clogs 're-tinned', as it was termed.

But no matter how new the boots or how good the stitching, water would find a way in. If not through the seams then over the tops! It is attributed to the 1st Duke of Wellington to have discovered 'high-tops' - what we now call 'Wellingtons' in his honour. Initially they were expensive. A cheaper way of keeping the feet dry was to attach wooden supports or iron stands called 'pattens' underneath the shoe with leather straps and so walk above the level of mud and mire. Although they were uncomfortable, cumbersome, and the cause of many a tumble and sprained ankle, they were so widely used, especially by women, that churches had a notice in the porch stating, "Ladies are required to remove their pattens before entering."

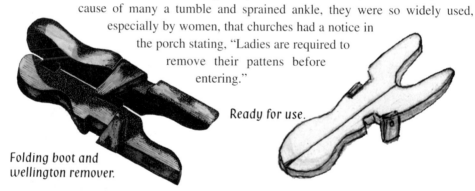

Ready for use.

Folding boot and wellington remover.

New boots were bought by the shepherd with the bonus on lambs dropped in May or June, by shearers from their piecework earnings in July, arable workers with their harvest wages in the autumn, and dairy and stockmen from their annual Christmas bonus. They wore their old and split boots in dry weather and saved their new boots for wet weather.

Wet boots were never dried by direct heat from a fire as that removed the oils and made the leather brittle and hard. A dish of chaff or bran was heated on the hob and poured inside instead. My mother made me stuff mine with old newspaper when I came home from school.

Until about 100 years ago all footwear was made straight to fit either foot. By alternating between left and right the wear was evened out and consequently they lasted longer. It was also impossible to put them on the wrong feet in olden days!

The coming of mass production caused a rapid decline in local shoemaking and cobbling. No longer did the worker have his own last. He had to wear boots that were not tailored to suit the odd shapes of his feet - some boots pinched and chafed with every step. But the countryman had his remedy. He soaked his new factory made boots in the river overnight to soften the leather, then wore them wet for work next day. The softened leather expanded around any painful pressure points of corns and callouses and when they slowly dried out in this way would forever after fit his foot like a glove - or should it be a sock? As they used to say, "Buy 'em, soak 'em, wear 'em and bear'em."

Boot and shoe stretcher.

And just think of it - if I hadn't had that bootscraper for Christmas I would have had to find something else to write about! So put your best foot forward into the New Year - but first make sure you clean your shoes before you go indoors!

58 February Threshing
NOISY MONSTERS WITH GIANT-SIZE APPETITES

How quiet the countryside sounds. Hard frosts and layers of snow serve to muffle the normal noises.

But it never seemed so silent in my younger days. For then the air echoed to the thrrrm-thrrrm-thrrrm of the mobile monster with an enormous appetite that could consume a whole corn stack in a few hours - the threshing machine.

Every day its melodious rhythm became louder as it threshed its way through neighbouring stackyards. Then late one afternoon the ground trembled as it trundled into our lane, trailing a black smoke screen that covered the cavalcade. The heavy traction engine, its spark guard aglow on top of the chimney, towed the large threshing box. Behind that the 'jackstraw' or elevator which in turn pulled the cart that contained all the essential bits and pieces, tools and spares. The elevator, box and engine were lined up in position between the first two stacks to be threshed.

Dusk had turned to darkness by the time the box and engine were sheeted up and the fire banked down for the night. About 6am the next morning the driver arrived on his bike, unsheeted the engine, livened the fire, emptied the ashes and stoked up to get a good head of steam ready for an 8 o'clock start.

Only the essential farm jobs were done - milking, feeding and mucking out - for there was always a lot of work to do before threshing could start. The thatch had to be taken off the stack and all the thatching pegs (broaches) accounted for, bundled and stored for next season. If the straw thatch was wet it was forked into a tumbril and tipped onto the midden to be turned into manure. If dry it was used to bed the bullock yards.

An occasional rat might be seen on the roof, suggesting a bit of sport later in the day. To comply with the law a couple of rolls of fine mesh wire netting were staked around the stack to stop them escaping.

Meanwhile the engine driver and his mate unsheeted the box, oiled and greased the shafts and bearings in a methodical manner, then unrolled long lengths of flat canvas belting. The wheels of the 'box' were chocked with wedges of wood, the shorter belt put on to the pulleys of the box and the elevator. The elevator was backed by hand and chocked when the tension was right. The big, broad belt was slung between the box and the traction engine. the engine reversed slightly taking up the slack and its wheels were chocked. All was ready!

Tumbril loads of best steam coal, collected from the station sidings, were piled nearby. A mobile 200 gallon galvanised tank of water on its three iron wheels stood beside the engine to quench its thirst, and a pile of buckets in case of fire!

Eight o'clock! A warning toot on the whistle, everyone stood clear of the main belt as the driving pulley was put into gear and the throttle gradually opened. Slowly the whole outfit resurrected into life. From the clattering of the metal belt joints passing over the pulleys and the vibration of other moving parts the experienced driver could tell immediately if anything was amiss.

The silence of a few moments before became a harmonious hum, the army of helpers - a hive of activity. Two men on the stack pitched the sheaves onto the top of the 'box'. There another passed them, one at a time and always with the ears in the same direction, to the chap who stood in the well beside the drum. He held a very sharp knife; it was also fastened to his wrist with a loop of binder twine as an extra precaution. When you've 'lost' one knife through the drum you never want to lose another! His job was to cut the string and feed the straw in a continuous stream into the rapidly rotating cylindrical threshing drum slightly beneath him, an art only accomplished after years of experience.

If the thatch had leaked or the sheaves had been stacked when wet, they tended to snatch through in lumps and the altered rhythm of the machine could be heard by all your neighbours who would know what condition the corn was in!

Periodically he collected a bundle of strings and passed them to the man below who tied the sacks.

The drum, rotating against the concave separated the straw from the grain and chaff. The grain fell further onto a fine sieve that sifted out any weed seed, poppies, cornflowers, etc. The corn was then elevated to the top of the machine where it passed through a smaller drum - an awner to remove barley awns - and fell on to a series of vibrating sieves that separated it into three grades: good grains, split and deformed grains and rubbish. Each flowed downwards through its appropriate chute into sacks suspended on iron hooks and standing on a flat door to keep them out of the mud.

As the sacks filled they were weighed off and the tops tied - into a mouth if secured around the neck, or into two ears if stitched along the top. They usually weighed one and a half hundredweights and were carted away on a sack truck or, if to be carried up the loft steps, they were lifted on to an upturned 40 gallon oil drum by the two men with the aid of a two foot bar. Each held one end of the bar against the base of the sack, which was leant on to the bar. The free hands caught hold of the sack's mouth or an ear and it was easily lifted horizontally on to the oil drum and pushed upright. Just the right height for one of the men to lower it onto his shoulders and carry it off - some two hundred journeys during the day - whilst the other man weighed the next bag and put an empty sack on the chute.

Oat and wheat chaff were also put into very large bags and tipped in the chaff house for future mixing with sliced roots for animal feed. Barley chaff contained awns - thin sharp one-way barbs that penetrated the skin and made you scratch and itch incessantly.

This chaff was usually dumped or put on to the midden.

After leaving the drum the good straw was jostled along walkers or shakers allowing any remaining grain to fall through. The straw eventually tumbled into the elevator whose two continuous chain link belts and spiked cross bars carried it aloft and dropped it on to the gigantic straw stack being constructed by three more men.

The worst job of all was shifting the puggle or cavings - short lengths of dusty straw. They usually put someone who was a bit lacking up top on this task but if he failed to turn up they used me instead - I don't know why?

Within minutes my nose would stream and my eyes became red, swollen and puffy, but the job had to be done - all day long. Forking it on to a large opened sack then carrying it by the four corners - as a bundled bag - to bed the bullocks, pigs, hens, cows and calves.

Apart from meal breaks my only relief was if the engine driver tooted his whistle. This was the signal for me to fetch more water, to quench the insatiable thirst of his engine. Bonnie the mare was already harnessed in the stable; she was soon hitched up and I was at the farm pit bucketing in gallons of ice cold water. Two blasts on the whistle meant "hurry up" and three, "what the hell are you playing at!"

Altogether a team of ten or preferably more people were needed to keep things running smoothly. During the War, ladies of the Women's Land Army took the place of the lads who were away fighting. German and Italian prisoners of war quite enjoyed a day away from their camp - they came complete with an armed guard. With neighbours, relatives, and lads home on leave, we usually mustered a good team.

As the day progressed the work got harder. Sheaves had to be lifted from the lower courses of the stack up onto the threshing box. Sacks in the granary were stacked three high and that last one took a lot of energy late in the day.

But there were compensations. It was the accepted custom to stop work to chase a rat and if several rats ran at once a yell would go up and everyone would join in the sport. Terriers, their stumpy tails wagging non-stop, would look under every sheaf as it was being lifted, in eager anticipation. Any rat was tackled with a nip in the neck, a quick shake, thrown in the air and the rat was dead.

Farm cats were never fed the night before threshing. They caught the mice and soon became so bloated and sick that they just watched them run away - to be swooped up by the barn owls at night. I always noticed many mice - few rats. Many rats - few mice. They didn't get on well together, even in a big stack.

Eventually the last sheaf came through, with a cheer from all the crew and the usual jocular remark - we ought to have started with that one!

The box and engine were sheeted up, belts put in the dry, the fire banked down, another day's threshing over.

Then it was only left to milk, feed the calves, pigs and bullocks, a good night's sleep, and an early start for the next stack tomorrow.

59 March Moles
BID TO ROUT OUT 'THE GENTLEMAN IN BLACK VELVET'

There is no doubt about it, March is the best month for catching moles.

Because so much of their life is spent underground few people ever see them alive. Usually the first indications of their existence are the characteristic tell-tale mounds of soil that suddenly appear around the house - or across an otherwise immaculate lawn!

And since most people are inclined to make "a mountain out of a molehill" there are dozens of remedies that abound for their removal; the list is as interesting as it is endless:

- smoke them out with fuses or squibs,
- gas them with lumps of carbide (acetylene),
- confuse their sense of smell with mothballs, nutmeg or burnt red herrings,
- clog their runs with tar, creosote, old sump oil or wet newspaper,
- injure them with broken glass, rose prunings or bramble pushed along their holes.

The Elizabethan gardener Thomas Hyll recommended the playing of football - the vibrations produced would scare them away. In a similar vein, one garden I used to pass on my way to school was full of clanking windmills sending vibrations into the ground! Another time-tested remedy is to bury bottles, their tops protruding just above ground level; when the wind whistles over them it makes them hum!

A slightly surer method is to plant leeks, onions or garlic around the boundaries. The best herb to keep them at bay is the 'mole plant': caper spurge, *Euphorbia lathrys.*

But there's only one sure cure - kill them and that's easier said than done.

Of the many traps that I have tried the scissor type is the most successful. Mole runs are usually four to five inches below the surface. To find them, the ground is prodded with a sharp spike **between** the mounds. A small square of earth is removed, surplus soil is cleaned from the tunnel on either side, the bottom levelled, the trap set and pushed into the hole. Daylight and draught are eliminated by putting grass, leaves or soil around the handles at the top of the trap.

Old pincer trap

The theory is that the mole will run along the tunnel, dislodge the central ring, spring the pincer claws shut and be killed quickly. But in practice it is seldom as simple as that. Perhaps the mole sees a shaft of daylight, feels a draught, smells the newness of the trap or scents the unfamiliar aroma of hands. He senses danger, burrows beneath the trap, fills it with soil, springs it, then heaves it out of the hole in revenge. Yes, they are cunning little creatures!

The professional molecatcher boils his new traps first, then buries them in the soil to remove the smell. Before handling them each day he washes his hands in a mixture of the blood and innards of dead moles, or wears gloves treated in the same way. The traps are also dipped into or smeared with the liquid. For if there is one thing a mole will not tolerate, it's another mole. They are ferocious and fearless and will fight to the death to defend their territories, except for a few **hours** each year between March and May when they mate. Female sows are as aggressive as the male boars and the scent of another mole in their run makes them throw caution to the winds and may cause them to lose their heads - in the trap.

Moles do not dig after each worm individually. Their territories consist of several hundred yards of tunnels which they patrol regularly on a shift system of roughly four hours on and four hours off - even at night, for the mole needs no lantern!

They hunt when they are hungry and when they are exhausted they rest in interconnecting underground chambers of grasses and leaves often called a 'fortress'.

Worms, centipedes, beetles, leatherjackets, spiders and slugs drop into the tunnels and are gobbled up by the next mole patrol! A mole eats its own weight (4 oz.) of worms (about 50) or the equivalent of other insects each day. If a surplus of worms is available the mole immobilises them by biting the nerves in their neck and stores them with some 100 others in one of many special underground larders ready for a rainy day - or severe frosts like we have had recently. Should the mole die of old age, at about four years, or be prematurely trapped, the stored worms will survive. The severed nerves gradually grow again and they can then make good their escape!

In wintry weather moles also burrow a secondary layer of tunnels about a foot deeper where worms are working or hibernating. Most of this soil is pushed to the sides of the tunnel; very little subsoil ever comes to the surface.

According to folklore, the majority of molehills are made on a waxing moon.

Moles breed from their second year onwards. They have their litter of three or four naked, pink, blind babies about June, in a nest under an extra large molehill - often up to a yard in height and diameter, and frequently built over a blind spring or underground watercourse. After a fortnight the youngsters grow a cream fur which changes to dark grey as they mature. They are then driven from the nest to colonise fresh areas. For a while they forage on the surface for carrion, worms, insects and small frogs. It is at this stage that they are most vulnerable to predators - foxes, badgers, owls, herons, stoats, weasels, dogs and cats. I remember we had one cat that brought so many moles home that we christened her "Moley".

Although dogs catch and kill moles they do not usually eat them. They roll on their backs over them instead. Why? I do not know! But what I do know is that the name 'mole' derives from the Anglo-Saxon *mouldewarp*, the 'mould-mover'. So efficient are its spade-like front feet at loosening the soil and its back feet in disposing of it - it moves 30 pounds of soil an hour -.that to excavate an equivalent amount for my weight I would have to shift 12 **tons** of soil an hour!

Shaped like a bullet, it can dig a hole and disappear from sight within 30 seconds. It can also construct 100 yards of tunnel in a day, which never needs to be shored up or braced. At that rate a mole could tunnel across the English Channel in just over a year, or since he is such a powerful swimmer, he might decide to swim across instead!

The highly appropriate collective noun for a number of these hardworking creatures is a 'labour' of moles - although they seldom stock heavier than three to the acre.

In 1702 a mole worked its way into our history books when a horse stumbled over its molehill. The rider, who was thrown and subsequently died was King William III. His Jacobite opponents were so delighted that henceforth they raised their glasses and in jest they toasted "the little gentleman in black velvet".

Because the waterproof fur can lie either way, it allows the mole to go backwards or forwards with equal ease. It is kept sleek and shiny by the high protein diet and constant rubbing against the tunnel walls. Country people discovered the hardwearing properties of moleskin trousers and waistcoats. Soon ladies of fashion used them to trim collars and cuffs and make gloves and muffs. The price of pelts rocketed. Farm workers found they could double or treble their low wages by catching moles in their spare time. Not only did the farmer pay them for all they caught, but good, thick winter pelts were sold in dried bundles to the furrier and there was a good market for dried feet!

Fore-feet worn round the neck were reputed to alleviate aches in the arms, and hind feet would cure cramp and rheumatism

Victorian spiked mole trap

Not widely used because the skins were of little value if punctured

in the legs. A whole mole held against the face eased the pangs of toothache.

Molecatching or killing them with an agonising dose of strychnine is still widely practised. Farmers object to molehills that smother good grass and at haymaking and harvest time blunt and break the cutting edges of knives, and spoil silage with gritty soil. Landlords make a particular point of this and my tenancy agreement instructs me to keep moles under control. To prove that I am fulfilling the terms of my contract I hang the corpses along the barbed wire fence for all to see

- and some to complain about! It's the modern variant of the gamekeeper's gibbet.

An Irishman once told me that there are no moles in his country because of their unusual method of exterminating them; they bury them alive! That one's good enough for April 1st! But what actually did happen to me one year on the first of April was that I found a dead sparrow in one of my underground moletraps. I was busy puzzling out how it could have got there when I heard roars of laughter coming from the nearby smithy! HE'D CAUGHT ME - I was the April Fool.

So, like those moles of mine - mind you don't get caught!

60 April Punishments

TAMING OF THE SHREW - BY DUCKING!

Many villages still have a set of stocks, a pillory, whipping post or circular lock-up. Preserved and listed as tourist attractions, their survival reminds us of some of the punishments inflicted on offenders in the past.

From early Saxon times until well into the reign of Queen Victoria, those caught breaking the rules of the community were subdued and shamed into repentance by the suffering and humiliation they endured during their punishment and the disgrace that followed them afterwards.

Stocks were used for minor offences such as thieving, dishonest trading and unruly behaviour. They consisted of two boards, hinged at one end and padlocked at the other, having holes into which the wrongdoer's ankles were secured. Some sets had two or three pairs of holes so that several people could be accommodated at the same time. Usually a seat was provided; if not, they sat on the cold soil for the allotted number of hours appropriate to their crime. Passers-by were encouraged to pelt them with mud, garbage and rotten eggs to add to their degradation.

I have heard of two unusual sets of stocks that contained five and seven holes respectively. In each case the odd hole was said to have been inserted to accommodate a one-legged man who regularly misbehaved. Warrington's stocks were on wheels so that malefactors could be towed through the streets, to their greater disgrace.

Pillories (from the French word meaning 'collar'), were mainly for men. They had to stand throughout their ordeal with their necks and wrists firmly fastened by the wooden collar. Their crimes were listed as forgery, perjury, cornering the market and so putting up the price of goods, and after 1637 illegal printing against the government. Vagabonds had to stand in them for three days and nights, during which time they were allowed only bread and water.

Adjacent to or part of stocks and pillories was a whipping post for dealing with more serious offences. The hands of the culprits were tied to it to prevent them escaping while they received the number of lashes ordered by the Justices. A local one is commemorated in the name of the pub at Peover - The Whipping Stocks. Vagrants caught begging or trying to settle in the area were whipped from village to village, from pillory to post ("from pillar to post"), to get rid of them.

Women were most frequently punished with water - by 'cucking' or 'ducking' stool. This was a mobile chair in which they would be fastened, first outside their own houses for pelting with rotten rubbish. Later they were paraded through the village and finally finished up at the 'ducking' pond. The chair was fastened to a long beam pivoted to a post on the bank. The accused was swung out over the water and lowered into the slimy depths repeatedly until she agreed to mend her ways. By this method many quarrels were quelled, tempers were cooled and shrews were tamed! (See picture p., chapter 78)

Macclesfield's contrivance is remembered in name by Cuckstool Pit Hill (near the station). Knutsford went one better, for they had two - one in high town and one in low town! Macclesfield also lays claim to have been the first town in England to use the 'scold's bridle' or 'brank' in 1623. This was a hinged metal-hooped headgear with a protruding plate that went into the mouth, held down the tongue and prevented talking (scolding). The husband had to lead his bridled wife through the streets on a halter for a set number of hours. Sometimes she was walked behind a cart instead.

In Congleton the Town Gaoler secured the scolding wife in the bridle and fastened her to a hook by the fireplace. There she had to remain until she relented, when the gaoler would be sent for to release her. The last report of its use was in 1824!

But the cruellest contraption of all can still be seen in the Stockport museum. Painted red, white and blue, the mouthpiece of this bridle had six sharp spikes on it, two pointing up, two down and two backwards. It must have inflicted terrible pain and injury on those forced to wear it.

The 'drunkard's cloak' was the remedy for revellers who had become over-intoxicated. They were stripped and made to walk the area wearing only the 'cloak' - an old beer barrel with holes for head and arms. Since everyone was free to ridicule and make fun of them they soon sobered up!

Village people were renowned for keeping a close watch on their neighbours. Anyone stepping out of line was warned, by sweeping their path and doorstep - to imply to the inhabitants to clean up their ways! A wife beater would have a bag of chaff emptied on his doorstep to signify "thrashing done within". A man married to a woman of loose morals might become the victim of a 'stag hunt'. The 'hounds', village men and boys with blackened faces, would empty a bladderful of bullocks' blood on his doorstep to display their disapproval.

Because a cuckoo lays its eggs in other birds' nests, husbands whose wives were adulterous were called 'cuckolds'. People would mock them by calling "cuckoo" every time they appeared.

An early, severe, punishment for adultery (which offended the Gods and harmed growing crops) was 'Riding the Stang'. The adulterer, astride a pole, was carried shoulder high through the village, then publicly burned alive whilst the onlookers hurled insults and missiles. In later times an effigy was carried and burned instead.

The guilty persons were identified by 'rough music' played by the 'rough band'. This was a procession of parishioners banging a rhythm on anything handy - pots, pans, pails and kettles. Each night they ended up at the adulterer's house and yelled and banged their condemnation until the adultery ceased or the terror-stricken persons fled the area. The last account I read of this actually happening was in the 1950s, only 30 years ago!

Frequently seen on the village greens are 'round houses', small circular buildings that served as temporary cells for petty offenders awaiting trial. Some had a portcullis of interwoven ironwork covering the doorway and windows; they were called 'cages' and the occupants were 'behind bars'. Those with no windows (wind-'eyes') were termed 'blind' houses and if the prisoners were fastened with chains, 'clinks'. There is an excellent example at Alton Towers.

Many of these ancient punishment sites of stocks, pillories, whipping posts and prisons were purposely positioned where the influence of natural (water?) forces imposed a delayed sense of subjection, dejection, gloom and doom on the subjects!!!

If they really worked as well as some people would have us believe, perhaps it's a pity they were ever allowed to die out?

61 May Ne'er Cast a Clout
A SWEET SMELL OF SUCCESS AS MAY'S RIDDLE IS SOLVED

I have always been intrigued by the expression, "Ne'er cast a clout until May is out." Does it mean don't discard your winter woollies until the hawthorn trees are white with blossom, or wait until the month of May is over?

At last I may have stumbled across the answer. It happened quite by chance while I was reading an old book on church customs in which the first Sunday in June is described as 'Sweet Sunday'. That set me wondering why.

History records, from the time of Queen Elizabeth I, that she and other wealthy people often had only **four** baths a year - whether they wanted them or not! In between times the rich masked their unpleasant smells with scents and perfumes.

Baths were even less popular among working people. They couldn't spare a special room in their already overcrowded homes to house such an unnecessary luxury. And as baths required so large a quantity of precious water to be carried to fill them, they washed instead - or at least sometimes.

It was once an annual event that soon after Michaelmas (September 29) children had their chests and backs plastered with a thick layer of goose grease. This was covered with a length of red flannel which was stitched in place. There it remained until the arrival of warmer weather the following year. One of the drawbacks, of course, was the smell. Goose grease and body odours combined to leave a lasting impression on all who ventured near them. But as almost every youngster was treated in the same way no one noticed anything unusual!

By my schooldays this practice had almost died out but I can well remember one autumn when the Medical Officer arrived to give us children a quick check over, he aroused the deep indignation of one mother who had her whole family of NINE children already stitched up in red flannel for the winter - but thankfully without the goose-grease!

Children were washed on the kitchen table. They stood in an enamelled bowl filled with water heated on the hob. A scrubbing brush was used to shift stubborn dirt, a rough flannel for the rest and a pumice stone for the thick-skinned. The ritual was always the same: up as far as possible, down as far as possible, and 'possible'!

Older members of the family washed from a bowl at the sink or used a hand scoop in the 'copper house' outside. Sometimes they sat for ages soaking their aching feet in a bowl of yellow mustard water to cure coughs and colds, purple potassium permanganate to alleviate the itches, salt water and lemon juice to cure chilblains or vinegar water to soften their corns.

After a day of dusty work haymaking, harvesting or threshing, the men would take a bucket of lukewarm water and wash themselves in the garden, screened from prying eyes by the row of runner beans which they watered at the same time. Nothing was ever wasted.

By the close of the last century no bedroom of distinction in upper class homes was complete without its washstand. On its marble top stood a large water jug inside its matching bowl. Beside it was a ceramic soap tray which had lots of holes to let the moisture drain through into the dish beneath, to keep the soap dry. Chamber maids filled the jug with hot water in the morning when they drew the curtains to awaken their 'ladies of leisure'. My mum had to come downstairs, boil her own kettle of water and carry it back upstairs herself, if she ever wanted to wash in private. One of the penalties of being a farmer's wife!

Gradually the message John Wesley had preached started to seep through to Society.

"Cleanliness is next to Godliness". The rich began to install bathrooms. Soon the mass production of lightweight zinc coated baths meant that they were within reach of poorer people's pockets, and being portable did not require a special room to accommodate them.

Working people bathed in front of the kitchen fire on the hearth rug. A couple of buckets of cold soft water were poured in; kettle and saucepanfuls of boiling water were added to increase the temperature. A small linen bag of oatmeal was squeezed in the water a few times, making it change to a lovely milky colour. It also hid the squiggling mosquito larvae from view. A few swishes and swirls with the wire mesh 'soap saver' that contained slivered remnants of used bars soon brought bubbles of softness to the surface. Towels steamed on the clothes maidens around the fire.

The youngest bathed first, sometimes two at a time. Then it was "Kiss everyone goodnight and straight off upstairs to bed with you or else you might catch cold through the opened pores of your skin." Sisters, brothers, grandparents, mum and finally dad all bathed in the same water, just a kettle full of hot added for each one, and yet dad came out as clean as the rest of us.

Again, nothing was wasted; next morning the now cold water was scooped into buckets, carried up the garden and poured into the celery trench. The green leaves stood out like oases surrounded by a sea of bubbles.

'Soft' water is rainwater, excellent for washing because it lathers so easily and requires no harsh detergents. Country people collected it from their roofs in barrels and butts, tubs and tanks, which were covered with wooden lids to stop the cats falling in. An old sock or stocking was pegged or tied to the bottom of the downspout. It filtered out some of the larger impurities - leaves, lichen and bird droppings!

In summertime the inside of these containers became smelly and were covered with a green slime which would rise to the surface in hot weather and sink before a storm. As a lad it was my job to scrub the sides and bottom of these when nearly empty and tip the residue away. This was always done during thundery weather or before the onset of rain so that the tanks would soon be filled again with a 'fresh' supply and the wooden barrels would not stand empty long enough to shrink and collapse, or leak when the rain did finally arrive.

If the tubs ran dry during a drought, washing water was fetched from the farm pond - tadpoles and all! Well water was for food preparation and drinking only.

My farm had the advantage of a piped water supply long before it came from the mains. We were supplied by a hydraulic ram whose thump, thump, thump went on continuously day and night. It used a lot of river water to compress air into a cast iron chamber. The back-pressure closed the inlet valve and sent a small but regular flow into the tank in the loft. One of the main drawbacks with this system was that when you had a bath you didn't always come out smelling of red carbolic or ashes of roses. Instead it was

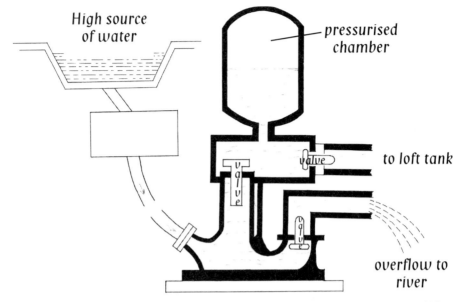

High source of water

pressurised chamber

to loft tank

overflow to river

whatever the farmer further upstream had just discharged in to the river, cowshed swillings or silage effluent!

However, coming back to the whole point of my ramblings, it is only in recent years that most people have had anything more than a good wash during the colder months of the year. Before this century they waited until the warmer weather arrived **after the end of May** before they washed or bathed themselves **thoroughly.** They got rid of their obnoxious odours, cast off their smelly winter clothes and put on fresh summer wear.

Thus they heeded the saying, "Button to chin till May be in, and ne'er cast a clout until May is out."

Which to my mind explains why the church used to call the first Sunday in June 'SWEET SUNDAY'! - that is, of course, unless you know of a better explanation?

62 June Memories
GROWING IN A COUNTRY GARDEN

There is an old Hebrew proverb that says, "As is the garden - so is the gardener."

In country districts it was once the custom that if a worker wished to change farms, the new employer, instead of asking for a reference, would go along to inspect the worker's garden. If he kept a tidy garden it was more than likely he would turn out to be a good worker and so was employed.

Cottage gardens were marvels of magnificence, labours of love and forestallers of famine. Lack of space meant that anything which served a useful purpose was packed in higgledy-piggledy as tightly as was possible for it to survive. If it didn't, another expanded to cover the space, yet annuals, biennials, perennials, herbaceous and bedding plants all grew happily together as a harmonious whole with seldom a bare patch between them.

The planting pattern in most country gardens was similar: a riot of sweet-smelling and picturesquely coloured flowers and shrubs at the front with the more mundane vegetable plot out of sight around the rear. Like my own, they were in many ways 'Gardens of Remembrance' - except that none of their plants were ever bought. They were begged, cadged or accepted as grateful gifts from neighbours, acquaintances and green-fingered friends. Each item had its story to tell, where it came from, when it arrived and how it survived. "This one from Mrs. So and So, that from up at the Hall, and the other from old xxx's now long since departed." The memories flood back each time their plant is tended - truly a 'Garden of Remembrance'!

Before the arrival of modern medicines many country housewives were well versed in the health giving properties of flowers and herbs. Their art was learned first hand at their mother's knee and later from the recipes in the family book of herbal remedies. Cordials, physics and purges tested by time and trial were added to and passed down through the generations on the female side. Children were taught to pick and prepare flowers, leaves, stems, bark and roots at specific times of the day, phases of the moon and seasons of the year. Then to dry, preserve, infuse, macerate or distil them into lotions and potions, pastes and pills, cordials and conserves. They were stored in bags and boxes, bottles and jars or just hung up somewhere dry until they were needed. Larger houses had a special room set aside for such preparations called a 'still' room (short for distil). Cottagers utilised their kitchens.

Pestel and mortar

Providing they were taken correctly, people using such homemade concoctions seldom suffered from the side effects that result from many of the synthetic medicaments of today. They usually worked well, provided the disease was not too serious or advanced and were often as good and sometimes better than many of the cures prescribed by the doctors of their day. The tendency was for people to concentrate on trying to remain healthy rather than curing illness. Consequently the plants they cultivated in their gardens were the ones they needed for their survival.

Rosewater was renowned not only for its sweet scent but also its healing properties. It turns out today that it is an antibiotic - as was the mould that grew on brown bread and cheese - a crude form of penicillin. The Romans knew about the cleansing power of lavender which gets its name from the Latin word *lavare*, to wash. They used it in their bathwater. It is a powerful antiseptic which kills fleas and lice. I use it as a hair oil, for it not only keeps the lice at bay but stops flies and midges biting me! It is also said to strengthen the hair - what little I have left. Sachets of lavender seeds placed in linen drawers kept moths away and smelt so much nicer than mothballs. An infusion of lavender tea helped against headaches, as did honeysuckle and willow. They all contain salicylic acid, the main ingredient of our modern aspirin.

Celery was the cure used for rheumatism; we used to grow it long and blanched in deep trenches which we filled with the cold bathwater - remember? Another aid for stiffness of the joints was to eat 'an apple a day', including skin, core and pips. This cured other complaints as well, including insomnia, for which to sleep on a hop-filled pillow was also highly recommended. "If agrimony is used instead, you will sleep as though already dead," runs the rhyme. Eating lettuces induced sleep and also slowed down your sex life.

Comfrey was called 'knitbone' because of its ability to bind broken bones together. A poultice was made of its pounded roots; it would set solid like plaster of Paris and encase the area. Gashes were healed by bruising and binding its fresh hairy leaves over the site. So successful was it in healing defects that promiscuous maidens would bathe in it before their wedding day to try to fool their future husbands into thinking they were still virgins!

After marriage, should a child not be forthcoming, leeks were given in large platterfuls to restore fertility. And when that happened raspberry leaf tea was the main drink for weeks beforehand to reduce the pangs of labour and childbirth.

Leek leaves macerated in vinegar for a day were the solution for corns. Applied over several consecutive nights it rendered them easy to remove. The juice from a fresh cut leek reduced both the pain and swelling from bee and wasp stings and would act as a fly deterrent.

Taken in small quantities rhubarb acts as a tonic but as you may well know from experience, too much will give you the trots! Housewives boiled it in furred pots, pans and kettles to remove the caked deposits of lime; and sticks of rhubarb dug into the soil stopped cabbages getting clubroot.

Similarly, the scent from marigolds killed nematodes and white fly. The small-flowered variety *Tagetes minuta* was particularly effective. Its power was known to the ancient Mexicans who dedicated it to their Goddess of Agriculture 'Mother Earth'. It also

helps other plants nearby to grow, especially potatoes and tomatoes, and is said to eradicate ground elder. I must try some on a patch I have.

From foxgloves we get digitalis, a heart stimulant. It also exudes the ability to keep plants around it healthy and improves the keeping quality of apples, pears, potatoes and tomatoes grown in the garden.

The presence of rosebay willowherb and parsley encouraged bees to hum and sing whilst pollinating the flowers of the garden, according to ancient annals. Should greenfly start attacking your roses, they suggested planting cloves of garlic

foxglove

beneath the bushes. They excrete a chemical into the soil which is drawn up by the rose roots and makes the sap unappetising to aphids! Onions and chives have a slower but similar effect.

On pests generally, the maxim was, "If it moves slowly, step on it. If it moves fast, leave it alone, it will probably kill something else." So the birds were left alone - and the blackcurrant bushes covered with cloths to stop them stealing the ripening berries.

It is perhaps a sobering thought that so many of the plants which still occupy a place of honour in our country gardens were once vital links in the chain of survival of our ancestors. In one of my old books it says, "The happier and more contented the gardener, the stronger the plants will grow, the more profusely the flowers will bloom and the heavier the fruit will yield." "A good gardener will improve a poor garden, but a poor gardener will spoil a good garden!"

Cottage gardens reflect the attitude and ability of the gardener - mine does get a bit cluttered up at times! Anyhow, I'm off to bed - I must have been eating too many lettuces!

63 July An Eye on the Weather
HOW TO KEEP YOUR EYES OPEN

There is an old proverb which says, "Only fools are weatherwise, and those that are are seldom otherwise!"

As a farmer the question I am most often asked is, "What's the weather going to be?" People assume that because I live and work so close to nature and the soil I possess some miraculous power to predict future weather patterns.

However, since my daily routine takes me out into the fields every few hours, I do have an advantage over others not so fortunate. For I am frequently reminded of some of the signs, symbols, sayings and secrets of weather-lore that are the culmination of centuries of experience by untold generations of observant country people.

Probably the best known saying is, "Red sky at night, Shepherd's delight. Red sky at morning, Shepherd's warning." This was in existence way back in Biblical times and a similar quotation by Jesus appears in Matthew 16, verses 2 and 3.

Our ancestors had to get the forecast right of their own accord; they had no professional weathermen on radio or TV to advise them. The output from a whole year of toil could be ruined by rain if the crop was cut at the wrong time. "Make hay while the sun shines" is as true today as when men first started to dry grass and conserve it for their newly-domesticated animals thousands of years ago.

So foolishly or otherwise here are a few of the many pointers that I take into consideration when planning my working programme.

Weather systems are constantly changing, and a belt of continuous rain seldom lasts very long - on average about four hours. So arose the saying, "Rain before seven, Fine before eleven." Thus a cloudy morning bodes well for a fine afternoon. A drizzle before breakfast at this time of the year is contemptuously referred to as the "pride of the morning." And if there is enough blue in the sky to patch a pair of sailor's trousers the sun will soon break through and shine.

wet weather

dry weather

A fall of soot into the living room grate or even the smell of it means either wet weather is on the way or my chimney needs sweeping - sometimes both! Similarly, should the drains smell they need cleaning out before nature flushes them out!

If my joints ache or my wife complains of shooting pains in her corns, I delay cutting my hay until another day.

Cockerels crow at dusk to herald rain by dawn, for the best rain falls at night. If rooks remain around the rookery, glide and circle water on their way to and from their feeding grounds or return late to roost, then rain is on the way.

Other wet weather indicators are bees hovering around the hive, cows collecting in a sheltered corner of the field all facing the wind, hens huddling tightly together; when water birds call, peacocks utter their shrill cry, frogs croak, sheep bleat and the missel thrush, nicknamed the 'storm cock', warns "more wet, more wet" from his perch on the topmost branch of the pear tree; the green woodpecker chuckles his laughing call, there is no dew on the morning grass, spiders spin short webs, the barometer falls when it is tapped and swallows fly low.

Yet more portents come from the plant world: the fallen fir cones that litter the churchyard drive close up tight to protect their seeds; dandelions, daisies and scarlet pimpernel close their petals to protect their centres; marigold, wood sorrel, trefoil and clover contract their leaves, and my holiday seaweed hanging by the back door swells and feels damp as its structure and its salts absorb the extra moisture from the air. The leaves of sycamore, poplar, lime and lilac turn and show the underside of their leaves.

Rabbits feed by day instead of during darkness; the blacksmith's anvil 'sweats' and droplets of moisture form - the bigger the drops, the heavier the forthcoming downpour! When the sound of distant church bells or railway trains, not normally noticed, can be clearly heard, then lift up your eyes. If you can see the hills, it's going to rain; if you can't, it's probably raining already!

It was once thought that cats could control the weather. If they washed behind their ears it produced rain. Dogs chasing their own tails or producing rumbles in their tummies was a sure sign of wind. Hence the expression, "raining cats and dogs" when there are heavy, driving gusty squalls!

The onset of wind is supposed to be foreseen by pigs, who will carry mouthfuls of straw around the sty. But always check first that it isn't just a pregnant pig building her nest before farrowing!

Mares tails

Strong winds are usually preceded by thin streaks of cirrus clouds high in the sky - their common name is 'mare's tails' because when they appear horses become restless, shake their heads, swish their tails, and their colts roll over and lie on their backs.

Summer storms are predicted by the storm-cock and flies that bite deep and painfully through socks and stockings - and if not swatted keep coming back for more. Gnats settle and suck blood, raising itchy bumps on bared skin. Partridges congregate into coveys and skim low along the crops and over the hedgerows.

Until recent years cattle would 'gad' - gallop around the field with tails erect - as the gad fly, the warble-fly now under eradication, laid its eggs under the hide covering their rear knee joints - a painful incision!

Bees become angry and will sting aggressively during stormy weather so beekeepers leave them alone until the calm which always follows the storm.

"When clouds appear like rocks and towers, the earth's refreshed by frequent showers." And those small clouds that scud along in front of the the larger, darker ones are called 'water carts' and will soon spill over!

In my house, a change in the weather is often indicated by the creaking of wooden beams, joists, floorboards and furniture as it expands or contracts in sympathy with the humidity, temperature and atmospheric pressure outside. This often coincides with a mottled mackerel sky, which means "never long wet, never long dry", if "long foretold - long last; short notice - soon past."

But the signs of good weather that I look forward to finding when I wish to make my hay are swallows flying high, spiders weaving larger webs, colonies of gnats that dance up and down in the evening sun, beetles that buzz around and bang into my lighted windows at dusk while bats flitter around the trees trying to catch them, heavy overnight dew that washes my wellingtons clean as I call my cows in for morning milking - and they take no heed and stay contentedly chewing their cud, obstinately refusing to rise until I reach them, then rather reluctantly they amble off towards the gate.

Meanwhile, swirls of morning mist in the hollows disperse, as the sun rises and gathers strength, or transfers themselves into a blue-tinted heat haze. My seaweed sample shrivels to a skeleton of its former self and the fir cones open to release their seeds. During the day fleecy clouds that look like tufts of cotton wool play an aeronautical version of noughts and crosses as they float between the long white vapour trails left by passing aircraft. And as I work in the fields making my hay, the countryside around is distorted into shimmering images as the reflected heat rises above the rapidly drying swathes.

All are signs of what the lyricists would call "those lazy, hazy, crazy days of summer" which, after our cold, wet spring, is just what the doctor ordered - and the parson prayed for!

Whatever we think of the weather, nature always balances everything out eventually, and the signs are always there for those who wish to use them. Recently I've been adding to the wisdom of weather lore by making a few additions to fit in with my haymaking:

"Evening red and morning grey - get out of
    bed and make your hay.
Evening grey and morning red - you might
    as well stay snug in bed."

The only drawback in my case is that whatever the weather I have to get up to milk my cows; and if it happens to be raining "cats and dogs", I usually issue a few proverbial words of wisdom on that subject too! But they are not printable here!!!

64 August Countryside Curiosities
WATCH OUT FOR A GOLDEN ORB IN THE SKY

During your 'sunny' summer holidays you may well be taking a trip around the country lanes, so I thought you might be interested in a bit of additional information about some of the items both familiar and unusual that you might see on your travels.

A few years ago a new water main was laid across my fields; in its wake have appeared several concrete monoliths! Where the pipe passed under the hedge is an upright post which simply states WATER. Close by are four small, squat, square notices: "S.V.", "H.", "W.O." and "A.V.". Ever wondered what they mean?

"S.V." is for Stop Valve, where the system can be turned off in an emergency, such as a burst, to avoid wasting water. "H" stands for Hydrant, which can be screwed into should a lot of water be required quickly - as in the case of a fire. "W.O." means Wash Out. Here a valve can be opened to flush away silt and sediment, and "A.V." is where an airlock in the pipe can be released. The signs also tells the size of pipe and its distance away.

Quite a common sight on our lowland grazing meadows are mass-produced galvanised or concrete cattle troughs. But when you get up into the hills a lot of those are hand-made of stone, hollowed out from a solid block of rock. Just imagine the hours of hard work and dedication that must have gone into chipping the inside out of each and every one of them. And also imagine the language that would result, if, having nearly finished, a fault was found and the stonework split into two!! These troughs are frequently set into the hillside and are fed with a supply of 'spring' water - which flows continuously throughout the year! They are found especially near the top and bottom of gradients and at staggered intervals up long slopes. They were purposely placed there, not just for the benefit of cattle that passed on their way to or from the fields or markets, but to act as sites where horses that had to pull heavy loads could stop and quench their thirst. When the age of steam arrived, traction engines used them to top up their tanks too.

In Victorian times they really went to town with troughs and produced some very attractive examples in stone, marble and cast iron. On top was usually a small fountain, its metal drinking cup fastened with a length of chain to prevent people taking it away. The fountain bowl overflowed into the horse trough below.

The most macabre water trough I have heard of was formerly a stone coffin!

I do know for a fact that many ancient stone fonts were sold as water or pig feeding troughs when they were replaced by the new polished marble ones which came into fashion in churches in the 1800s! Nowadays these old fonts and fountains, troughs and early earthenware sinks have been given a new lease of life and are highly prized as flower containers.

Beside the road or near the edge of a village green you may come across a hole where you can go down one or two steps to a supply of running water. These 'waterspouts' once provided village people with clean washing water. Drinking water was usually hauled up from a well with bucket and windlass. Few of these remain, except in ornamental form - as wishing wells.

Much more frequently found are village pumps. Every day the country housewife had to crank the creaking weighted handle to draw enough water for the needs of the household. She carried it home in heavy wooden buckets, balanced by and suspended from her shoulder yoke, which took away some of the strain.

A later innovation for pumping larger quantities was the water windmill. High on its tapered scaffold frame, the rotating vanes lifted and lowered the pumping plunger sending thousands of gallons daily into large storage tanks. These would keep the users supplied during spells of calm weather when there wasn't sufficient wind to work the sails.

And have you ever wondered why the four long angled arms that operated the corn grinding windmills came to be called sails? It was because the wooden framework was covered with 'sail' cloth. On very windy days the sailcloth had to be partly furled to prevent the sails gathering too much momentum. The main disadvantage of this method was that each sail had to be stopped vertically in turn. The miller had to climb aloft and fasten the sheet to the framework according to the strength of the wind - a difficult, dangerous and time-consuming task.

In the course of time, hinged wooden shutters were introduced and the driving force of all four sails could be altered immediately without halting the grinding process by operating a lever inside the mill. Later this was done automatically, but the rotating arms are still called 'sails'!

Along the side of the main road and half hidden by my hedge is a 'milestone'. As its name suggests, they were formerly made of stone but are now frequently found in variations of flat, triangular or rounded cast iron, with the distances to main centres of life along the route given in 'miles'. The word originates from the Roman *mille* - one thousand paces of two strides - equivalent to about 1680 of our present yards. The mile of 1760 yards which we use today was fixed in the reign of Queen Elizabeth I. But many old milestones still give their distances in Roman numerals!

At road junctions 'signposts' were formerly called 'fingerposts' because they *pointed* the way. They were set at the head height of a person riding on horseback so that he could read it easily - people who travelled on shanks's pony (on foot) were considered largely illiterate. Many a traveller - like myself - has strayed miles along the wrong road because some local prankster had rotated these signs in the opposite direction!

At the end of country lanes, or by farm entrances, you may see a platform raised two or three feet above the road. This was a 'churn stand' where the farmer used to leave his milk for collection in the days before the large round milk tankers took it away in bulk. If you've never noticed one, have a look at mine next time you are passing. It is just beside the road, built of stone and set into the hedge bank, right next to my farmhouse. The postman and delivery men come up to the steps beside it to reach the path to my door.

Which leads me on to another relic of our 'horsy' heritage - 'upping blocks'. These consist of two or three large stone steps climbed by the less agile to make it easier to mount their steeds. They also saved ladies, who always rode sidesaddle, the embarrassment of employing the hostelier (ostler) to help them mount. These 'mounting blocks', as they were also called, were used by people dismounting from horses, coaches and carriages as well, and are still found where people congregated - by churches and inns.

Before the introduction of kerb stones, stone bollards were placed at corners to stop carriage and wagon drivers 'cutting the corners'. In towns they helped to prevent the wheels mounting the pavement and running over people's feet. Similarly, boulders were placed along the base of buildings to prevent the wheels damaging the walls and to give pedestrians a refuge from runaway coaches or bad drivers. Bulging walls were buttressed with brick or stone to stop them collapsing completely.

On the walls of some houses you may see an old 'hay cratch'. Formerly used for feeding hay to horses, it now contains a colourful profusion of flowers. So great is the demand for them that my local blacksmith makes more now than he ever did for horses!

Another interesting object to look out for is the great golden orb that is sometimes seen as it glides across the sky during daylight hours. The older ones amongst us suggest that it was spotted far more frequently in the days of our youth. In some seasons it is so rare that it is seldom seen at all. When it does manage to shine through the gloom it only lasts for a few fleeting hours. So if you do happen to catch a glimpse of it, make the most of it - because it may not last long! Happy holidays!

An unusual Victorian six-sided letter box for postcards home from your holiday resort.

65 September Getting the 'Sack'
WHEN FARM WORKERS REALLY GOT THE 'SACK'

As flocks of Canadian geese arrive to spend the winter with us, swallows congregate ready to leave on their long migratory journey to the warmer climes of Africa.

Trees take on an end of season haggard look before their green tones change into the colourful tints of autumn. The chill wind that has been with us all summer develops into a definite nip at night. The first frosts arrive to blacken the gale-torn remnants of the runner bean rows and to turn the delicate borders of bedding plants into a mulchy mess.

Summer - or what little we have had of it this year - is over. Autumn has arrived. It is the season of Michaelmas. This once-famous festival is now noted by very few, for modern times and methods have changed the priorities of working people. No longer does the Feast of Michaelmas conjure up happy memories of countryside hiring fairs that were long linked with it.

It all started because a plague known as 'the Black Death' wiped out so many people that skilled workers were at a premium. The survivors asked for and received higher and higher wages. To combat this escalation, a law enforced all able-bodied men to offer themselves for hire at a fixed wage. Magistrates were empowered to fix the rate annually and make it known at the Statute Sessions - held at Michaelmas in particular.

Farmers and workers gathered to hear their new rates of pay and conditions of service and many entered into hiring agreements on the spot. Because lots of people attended, they needed sustenance - and shrewd stallholders set up shop to satisfy their needs. Next came entertainment. Soon the session occupied the whole of the holy-day (in Latin-fair) so it became a hiring holiday or hiring fair.

Although the statute ceased in the reign of Queen Elizabeth I, the formerly serious sessions had by then been transformed into a happy holiday atmosphere which was allowed to continue.

Since Michaelmas marked the end of harvest and the beginning of the cultivation for next year's crops, if either a farmer or a worker were dissatisfied with the other this was the ideal time to seek a change. Thus the question that was currently on everyone's lips was, "Are you staying on?" The way the farmer made it known to one of his men that his services were no longer required was to present him with a SACK. Into this the worker bundled his tools and belongings and left for the hiring fair. When asked by his workmates, "Are you staying on?" he would simply reply, :No, I've got the SACK!"

The reason that workers left the farm was not usually to better themselves or get more money, for wages were universally controlled. It was because the farmer had a bad temperament or didn't feed them well enough.

Unmarried employees from about 13 to 30 years 'lived in'. Girls slept in the house, men in the stable or cowshed lofts. All ate together in the farmhouse. If the farmer's wife was stingy with the food, or simply a bad cook, that farm usually had a high turnover of staff. Farmers that provided the best 'tables' not only kept their workers but also had a waiting list.

If women sought to go into service at the hiring fair they would wear a piece of mop in their cap, hence the name Mop-Fair! Men would wear a woven plait or token denoting their trade and competence. A wagoner wore a length of leather whipcord, farmworkers circles of plaited straw, tied with a tuft of wool for a shepherd, strands of cowhair for a cowherd or horsehair for a ploughman. The number of circles gave the wearer's grade, one - first class, two - second class. Those falsely showing an ability above their status would soon be put into place by the men at their next job if they couldn't perform their duties up to standard.

At some fairs hopeful hands stood waiting in rows for inspection by the farmers during the morning. At others they wandered around looking for a likely employer. Most farmers and men within a district already knew one another, if not by personal knowledge, by reputation However, should a strange farmer approach, he would ask who they had worked for, how long, and why they were leaving. After a short chat, he might say, "Right'o, I'll go and see So and So and get your character."

On his return, the strange farmer said, "Yes, you've got a good character, I'll take you on."

"Ah," said the man, "and I've also got yours and I bain't a'coming...!!!"

There is also the tale of the Cheshire lad who, when asked why he had left his former farm, said, "Well, sir, one day the cockerel died, the master went indoors, took some salt from the saltbox and sprinkled it over the dead bird. Next day we had it for dinner."

"Nothing unusual in that," said the farmer, "I do the same on my farm as well."

"Yes, sir," said the lad, "but soon afterwards one of the master's pigs died, the master went indoors, took some salt and sprinkled it over the pig and we lived on that pig for weeks afterwards."

"Nothing unusual in that either, my lad; if you came to work for me the same thing would happen - we don't waste anything in the countryside."

"Yes, sir," said the lad, "but last night the master's wife died, he came downstairs and fetched some salt - and she's a tough old begger and that's why I'm here sir!!!'

If the farmer and worker agreed that they were suited the bond was sealed with a 'fastenpenny'. (Later a sixpence and this century a shilling). The worker spat on it for good luck as it signified the 'earnest' promise of more money to come. They shook hands and the employee started work on the farm next day, unless it was a Friday, Saturday or Sunday since they were unlucky, as was New Year's Day in Cheshire! Should either or both be dissatisfied after a few weeks, there was a second chance to be had at the smaller 'Runaway Mop Fairs' held on St. Martinmas Day - November 11th.

If the man or woman was employed to work in their own parish the duration of the agreement was for the full year. Outsiders were only taken on for 51 weeks. This was so that they couldn't claim to be established parishioners and therefore were not entitled to dole, poor rate, or any other charity 'on the parish'. Most hirings were completed by the end of the morning.

Thrifty youngsters would spend some of their yearly earnings on clothing and new boots to allow them to walk dry shod during the winter. A watch had always to be kept for confidence tricksters who would try to tempt young country simpletons into buying a pig in a poke (sack). Some lads fell for it, others remembered their parents'

advice and poked the pig first to hear if it squealed. One lad opened the sack to see the so-called 'pig' inside but by so doing 'let the cat out of the bag'.

They all tried hard to enjoy themselves while it lasted. Lads and lasses eyed one another up as they danced to the music of flutes, fifes and fiddles. Some blew a whole year's hard-earned wages away during the day on wine, women and song. As they say, "Easy come, easy go."

As the day wore on, both the merriment and the drunkenness increased, squabbles and fights broke out, sometimes leading to disgraceful scenes and riotous behaviour. It all meant extra business for the Justices of the Peace, clerks, parish officers - and later midwives for miles around. Old church records show that many a damsel in distress asking 'parish relief' for her illegitimate child claimed that her ruin arose from attending the

Michaelmas Hiring Fair!

Slowly but surely the importance of the hiring fair began to diminish. There were many contributing factors:
- the enclosure of common lands
- the gradual drift of low-paid countryworkers into higher-paid prospects in the town
- factory owners trying to discipline their workforce to factory hours and holidays
- better education and communications
- the agricultural depressions
- and finally, the carnage of a generation of young workers in the First World War.

In the passage of time, the Michaelmas hiring fair was succeeded by the 'Labour Exchange', which in turn has been replaced by the High Street 'Job Centre'. Judging by the large numbers who still remain unemployed after mid-day, I often wonder if we've lost something in the process?

<h2>66 October Words that 'Count'</h2>
<h2>HIDDEN PAST OF THE WORDS THAT COUNT</h2>

Lingering in our language survive several snippets of interesting information that are still in use as everyday expressions. Often we do not realise the important part they played in the progress of our evolution or the context from which they were taken. Here are a few examples.
- What's the SCORE? Ask the EXCHEQUER.
- It's bound to be ONE or the OTHER - but it doesn't TALLY.
- Take STOCK, STOCK-take and STOCK-pile.

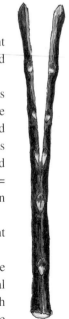

Have you spotted the link between them? They are all connected with ancient methods of counting, some as old as the hills, or certainly the sheep that roamed freely upon them.

The primitive way of counting was on the fingers, which the Romans called DIGITS. The first four were written as upright fingers: i, ii, iii, iiii (the dots representing the nails?). Five was the outline of the whole hand simplified as a 'v'. Six was a whole hand and a finger (vi), and so on up to ten, which was two hands crossed: 'x'. Later four (iiii) became one (i) less than five (v): iv, and nine one less than ten: ix. Major numerals were replaced by initial letters: 50 = L, 100 = C, 500 = D, 1000 = M. So can you work out MCMLXXXVI seen on some book and film titles this year?

Although the Romans counted in tens, our Anglo-Saxon ancestors went one better and used both hands and feet to count in twenties! Here's how:

In the days when farm animals were sold at the 'hiring fairs', they were purchased by 'drovers' who walked them on long journeys to their final destination. Frequently the farmer didn't get paid until the drovers returned with the money. Neither the farmer nor the drover was able to read or write, but the number of animals involved was recounted weeks later by notches cut into a stick.

Until quite recently along the Scottish borders and Lake District, animals, especially sheep, were counted into twenties in variants of the Celtic language. One goes: "Yan, Tan, Tethera, Methera, Dic; Sezar, Lezar, Catra, Horna, Tic; Yan-a-tic, Tan-a-tic, Tether-a-tic, Mether-a-tic, Bub; Yan-a-bub, Tan-a-bub; Tether-a-bub, Mether-a-bub, Gigget."

Now Gigget was 20 animals, so a stick was notched or scored with a knife; another 20 animals counted, another SCORE on the stick; and that is how 20 became a SCORE. Odd animals were notched on the reverse side of the stick. The farmer signed his mark, an 'X', the sign of the cross, which he kissed as a bond.

The stick was split into two, lengthwise, dividing all the marks. The farmer kept one half of the stick, the drover the other. When final payment came to be made, the two halves were put together and they had to TALLY.

The system was fairly foolproof. It was no use a dishonest farmer adding an extra notch to his half, because it wouldn't have a corresponding notch on the other half, and therefore wouldn't tally! And of course the drover couldn't reduce his payment to the farmer by removing a notch to "settle an old score"!

Because similar notches were once cut into sticks to count the runs at cricket or the goals in football, we now ask, "What's the SCORE?"

When counting large herds and flocks through tollgates the keepers found it too time consuming to notch sticks. They counted 20 pebbles into a pocket for every 20 animals that passed through. This tradition is still carried on today by cricket umpires, who transfer a pebble or marble into their pocket for every ball bowled in the 'over', until the sixth is reached!

When I was a lad all our eggs were sold at the market, not by the dozen, but by the SCORE. Before metric measures were introduced my pigs were always sold by the SCORE (20 lbs). And according to the Bible my average life expectancy is three SCORE years plus ten, which should leave me enough time to write about another 150 articles!

"The king was in his counting house, counting out his money" runs the nursery rhyme. The method he used for calculating the royal revenue was a chequered cloth or table. It was in use over 900 years ago, was later presided over by the Treasury and not abolished until 1833! Which is why the Minister originally in charge of the chequered cloth method of counting money is now known as the EXCHEQUER.

Until 1826 money loaned to the government was recorded on square sticks. Notches on one side acknowledged the sum paid; on the opposite side were written the date and the name of the payer. Notches and name were split into two longitudinally. The EXCHEQUER kept one part, the counterstock; the donor was issued with the other, the stock, as evidence of the King's debt.

When repayment was required the STOCK was exchanged for money in the building called the STOCK EXCHANGE. Those unable to present their stock personally employed someone to do it for them - a STOCKBROKER.

Because of the increasing number of transactions, the system became clogged; it was too slow and cumbersome and took up too much space. So in 1826 a change was made to recording with pen and paper. Eight years later the accounts were up to date. But what was to be done with the masses of now obsolete wooden stocks? It was eventually decided to use them as firewood. In 1834 so many were put into the stoves of the 'House of Lords' that they overheated and started the fire which burned down the old Parliament buildings!

Even stranger perhaps is the fact that in Anglo-Saxon times 'stocks' meant sticks or logs. A man's wealth was estimated by the size of the woodpile he had accumulated - STOCKPILED - which was a guarantee of his comfort in the cold weather to come. Which is why, once a year, those in business still take STOCK or STOCK-TAKE.

The servant employed to fuel the fires with wood was a STOCK-ER, now abbreviated to STOKER.

When I started farming, every bag of corn I carried up the granary steps was accounted for by a vertical pencil mark on the whitewashed wall - until four were in a row. The fifth mark crossed them diagonally, so yet again they could be counted in multiples of five and reckoned in scores.

An old quarry I visited regularly had two peg boards of 20 holes. A peg was put into the first board every time a load was removed. When all 20 holes were filled, a peg was put into the second SCORE-BOARD and the first board cleared. By this simple system of 'SCORING' 420 loads could be recorded - more than they needed in a month of Sundays!

Before 1066 items numbered in order were first, OTHER, third, fourth, etc. This was so confusing that a French word was 'borrowed' which has since become our 'second'.

Our present 'Arabic' numerals, 1, 2, 3, 4, 5, originated in India over a thousand years ago. Through commerce they spread via the Moors and Spaniards into England. Their importance was that columns to the left indicated units, tens, hundreds, thousands, using the same nine basic numbers. For 600 years the Roman and Arabic systems were used side by side. The big breakthrough came when a 'nought' was added to the Arabic system, giving us the ten numbers we use today.

During all this time the Chinese, Egyptians, Greeks, Romans and Russians had perfected the Abacus - rows of coloured beads on wires - like we had in our play pens as children. With practice, their accountants can achieve speeds equal to our electronic calculators!

But the way farming has been going downhill lately I don't need a calculator or an abacus to count my profits. I can do it on my fingers - on ONE hand!

67 November A Pig's Life of Luxury
WHEN PIGS LIVED A LIFE OF LUXURY

Dearly Beloved Brethren - isn't it a sin,
That when you peel potatoes - you throw away the skin;
The skin feeds the pigs, and the pigs feed you;
Dearly Beloved Brethren - isn't that true?

There was a time when the pig was the most commonly domesticated animal in this country. Almost every cottager kept at least one. The usual way of obtaining a young pig was from a local farmer. If you helped him to gather in his hay you would be repaid at the end of the following winter with a weaned piglet. If you helped him to gather in the corn harvest as well, you could have two! So initially they cost nothing, apart from a few hours of hard work.

The new piglet became the focus of attention in the household and quickly adapted to its life of luxury. A box of hay was placed near the fire to keep it warm at night so that it didn't pine unduly for its mother. Tempting tit-bits of food and milk were offered to it and usually within a day or two it would scoff anything fed to it.

Children found it an ideal pet and under their gentle care it became completely docile. It would allow itself to be dressed in baby clothes, wrapped in blankets and pushed and paraded around the village in the little pram, like a living doll. Or pulled along in the boys' soap box cart, to the envy of all the other children in the area.

For a short while it had complete freedom to roam, indoors and out. Often it slept with the children for, surprisingly, pigs can be very clean creatures! They are as intelligent and affectionate as most dogs and can be trained to do tricks, retrieve, obey commands and harnessed to pull children around in their carts. When young and free they had a bell hung around their necks to help them to be found.

But sooner or later the inevitable happened. The piglet, growing rapidly in size and curiosity, would start to root up the garden, tip over a bucket or make a mess in the house. That was it, enough was enough! "It's the sty for you from now on," said Mother and Father.

Fortunately, the children's caresses were now centred on a cuddly cade lamb - the novelty of the piglet had worn off. So, except for a few harnessed outings pulling them around in the cart, the low-roofed, draught-proof sty with its deep bed of clean straw became its new home. There it would thrive and constantly root the straw around and toss it into piles.

But there were disadvantages. The pig no longer found its own green food. It all had to be collected by the family. Every day baskets and buckets, saucepans and sacks were filled with nourishment. From the field and hedgerow - hogweed and sowthistles, dandelions and docks, comfrey and chickweed. From the garden - anything surplus and edible, caterpillar-holed cabbage leaves, lettuce stumps and carrot tops. From indoors - into a bucket under the sink was poured any cold tea, vegetable straining water, crusts that grandma and grandad couldn't tackle because they had no teeth! Stale bread and cakes (very rare!).

In spring when hens were incubating, into the bucket went infertile eggs, discarded shells, dead and malformed chicks - all sank into the dark watery depths. Washing-up water made up the bulk of the liquid, for chemical detergents were unknown, only natural animal fat soaps. Also added - as in the opening poem - were potato peelings and pig 'taters - little ones too small to peel and larger ones damaged by slugs, frost or blight. Boiled on the hob, they warmed the contents of the bucket. To this slop was added a bit of barley meal; sometimes the mixture thickened into a mash, sometimes it remained sloppy.

Yet, however presented, it was greedily gobbled up three times a day, morning, noon and night - plus the greenstuff!

A fresh sod of turf daily gave the pig something to play with, whilst an occasional handful of small coal or cinders stimulated its flow of saliva and aided its digestion.

Wooden troughs were ridged where countless tongues had worn the soft wood clean away searching for the last morsel; the harder grain and knots stood out in polished relief. Metal troughs were licked bright and black. As the pig's snout grew in strength, these lighter and lower troughs were bumped and clattered around the sty; they had to be removed. From then on the pig was fed in the immovable higher and heavier stone trough instead.

The method of feeding was vitally important. Too much food given too early in life would produce internal fat and impede future growth. The secret was to supply it with just sufficient to grow rapidly, then give it as much as it could eat in the final stages - to finish fattening.

If you didn't feed the pig enough when it was growing it became bored and restless. Sooner or later, it would find a loose brick or cobblestone in the floor. This it would nudge and nurture incessantly until eventually it came out. Then the pig entered into its seventh heaven. In would go its strong snout to root around the hole until another was heaved out - then another and another. By evening half the sty floor would be uprooted!

There was only one remedy. Down to the blacksmith's to get some pig rings - cruel-looking horseshoe nails, hammered flat and spiked, sharp at both curved ends. The pig's nose was noosed behind the incisor teeth and the rope tied to the rafters. With the pig pulling backwards and squealing to high heaven, one ring was closed through the skin above each nostril with the curved pliers.

Silence reigned! It was all over except repairing the sty floor. The pig settled down to its normal routine of eating, sleeping and rubbing itself on its itching post - the certain sign of a satisfied pig.

Everyone who came to visit would enquire after the pig - it was considered very bad manners if they didn't! This was followed by a walk up the garden path, admiring and praising the growth of the vegetables on the way, ending up at the sty. Then there would follow a long and deep discussion on the pig's merits, its conformation, future feeding, and COST. For as the pig increased in size, so did the amount of barley meal it required. By late summer nearly half the husband's wages had been spent on buying food for the pig; by late autumn, three quarters!!! Household economies had to be made. Indeed, it was often said that many a cottager lavished more care and attention on his pig than he ever did on his wife!!!

However, as the leaves blew off the trees and supplies of fresh greenstuff became scarce, new items were added to the pig's menu. Barley meal was supplemented with windfall apples and nothing improves the flavour of a pig as much as a little apple on your pork! Acorns were collected by the bushel; although poisonous in quantity to cattle, they were quite harmless to pigs. They would put a couple of inches of EXTRA fat on the pig in its last few weeks. But what a backbreaking and tedious task it was collecting enough every day. Soon there were no more to be had. The cold winds of winter were starting to whistle through the cracks. The acorns were all eaten. The sack of barley meal was empty. It was the day of decision in the household.

For the best part of the year the family had made sacrifices in time, effort and money to enable their pig to lead a life of luxury, to be fed and to be fattened. Now it was time for him to repay the debt and feed them.

68 December Killing the Cottage Pig
ONLY THE SQUEAL IS WASTED AS A
'PET' REPAYS A DEBT

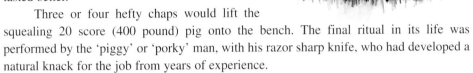

The 'killing' of the cottage pig was traditionally done at the time of a waxing moon - to prevent the meat shrinking - and on a Friday, because in ancient times the pig was sacrificed to the Celtic Goddess Freya after whom the day was named - unluckily for the pig!

It was essential that the pig was starved for at least a day before it was slaughtered, otherwise the meat might not keep. A 'clemmed' pig also tasted better.

Three or four hefty chaps would lift the squealing 20 score (400 pound) pig onto the bench. The final ritual in its life was performed by the 'piggy' or 'porky' man, with his razor sharp knife, who had developed a natural knack for the job from years of experience.

The blood was caught in a large basin and would coagulate to form the basis of black puddings. The pig, now still and silent, was rolled on to the 'ladder' and transferred into the 'turnel' - a special wooden bath. Buckets of hot water were thrown over him; he was scrubbed clean then vigorously scraped. His bristles were bundled for use by the brushmaker and a few were saved for the cobbler. The horn casings of the cloven trotters were clawed off; local lads would chew the softer parts, then discard the harder horn to be eagerly eaten by the dogs.

The back legs of the pig were fastened to a curved notched stick called a 'cambril' and it was hoisted aloft - ready for the pig to be opened up. The innards contained too much for one family to eat immediately, so children were sent running on errands to distribute the tasty bits and pieces among favoured friends and neighbours - a compliment that was always returned when they killed their pig.

Boys waited anxiously for the bladder. When drained, it was blown up through a hollowed elderberry stick or a piece of broken pipe stem. The neck was tied with thin string to stop the air escaping and off they scampered, bouncing it aloft as a balloon, or kicking it as a football.

Once the innards were removed, that was all that could be done for now to the still-warm carcase of the pig. It was carried to the outhouse and hung from the central beam's sharp spike through its lower jaw - the overnight resting place of many before it and quite a few thereafter. A stick held the belly flaps wide open to allow the air to circulate and cool it evenly.

Peace reigned in the darkness outside, but indoors was a hive of noise and activity. Grandmothers, mothers, daughters, friends and relations, were all busily helping to prepare the various parts. Children turned the entrails inside out on a stick and washed them clean.

When soaked in salt water for three days the smallest were plaited and fried as 'chittlings'. Medium-sized ones might become sausage skins and the largest would contain black puddings.

Pig scraper and trotter horn remover

Grannies and neighbours cut the flear - the stomach fat - into small cubes which, together with a sprig of rosemary, were rendered down into lard in saucepans over the blazing fire. They continually poured the melted fat into basins and jars, or sometimes utilising the bladder as a container and pouring the hot fat in through a funnel. The residue of the flear was fried into 'scratchings'. Meanwhile, mother was chopping pieces off the heart, liver, lights (lungs) and sweetbreads, mixing them together with fat to make a supper of delicious 'fry'. The whole cottage was filled with the smell of pig fat and a blue haze hung in the air.

Younger children did not realise that all the commotion - and their sudden increase in fatty food - came as a direct result of the death of their former pet. Older ones, torn by the sadness and sorrow of their pig's untimely and undignified end, eventually decided that a full stomach was more satisfying than empty sentiments.

Everyone slept soundly that night. Next day the now-cold carcase was cut up. The head was removed, cut into two, and the brains put into a basin. The backbone cut away and divided between the helpers to bake into sweet 'backbone pie'. 'Faggots' - also called 'savoury ducks' or 'poor man's goose' - were fashioned from the liver, fat pork, onions and herbs. They were rolled into balls and cooked wrapped in the lacy stomach lining called the 'caul' which left decorative patterns on the outside.

The pig's feet were boiled and the liquid was poured into earthenware basins crazed with age. When cold and set it became 'trotter jelly'. Each foot was a meal in itself, chewing the meat and gristle from the multitude of small bones on the trotters. Greasy fingers were wiped on trousers, waistcoats or aprons - or simply licked clean, for they had no knowledge of napkins!

The head, ears, tail and scraps were boiled with peppercorn and herbs until the meat fell away from the bone. The meat was finely chopped, mixed with sage, nutmeg and pepper according to taste, then made into a sloppy mixture with some of the liquor. While still warm it was pressed into greased basins and a weighted plate put on top. When cold and set it was turned out like a jelly - 'brawn' - all ready to be sliced.

Hams and bacon were rubbed with salt and saltpetre then pickled in a salt solution (brine) strong enough to float an egg. They were turned daily so that all was evenly salted. After several days they were removed, covered with butter muslin and hung to dry from

cambril

ceiling racks or wall hooks. Some of the hams and bacon might also be hung from the beam that crossed the chimney - as in my house. There they slowly absorbed the smoke from the wood fire below until they were 'cured' - not that they had ever been ill!

But pork does soon go off - especially in hot weather, which is why in olden days it was never eaten unless there was an 'R' in the month. Another problem is that pig meat is very close-grained and not easily digested by everyone. But most country people used it up as fast as they knew how. Pork pies, pork cheeses, pork sausages or just plain pork sliced from 'cut and come again' joints. Thick or thin, boiled or fried. Made into roly-polys with dumpling and bacon all cooked together in a stocking! Mixed with potatoes and baked in a crusty 'clanger' full of nourishment, not half-empty like the pasties on sale today.

Country people were often nicknamed 'Chewbaconers'! They liked their bacon served in soup plates - swimming in fat! Fat was used for cooking, making candles and rushlights. Even when rancid many uses were found for it - as axle grease, to rub on sharpening sticks to hold the sand in place; and nails and screws dipped into it didn't rust as fast. Lard became an essential ingredient of many lotions and haircreams, as well as flaky pastry and lardy cakes. Actors who used ham fat for removing greasepaint became 'ham actors'!

Pig-skin can be used as leather; if not, when it is cooked the skin on bacon becomes the 'rind' and on pork the 'crackling'. Indeed, it was often said of the pig that only the squeal ever escaped - and that only because no use could be found for it - until someone invented pneumatic lorry brakes!

The cottage kitchen-cum-living room was a sight for sore eyes at Christmas time. On the open storing racks suspended from the ceiling were the hams that had been pickled. Their thick crustations of crystalised salt sparkled as brightly in the warmth of the flickering firelight inside, as the frosted snow did in the cold moonlight outside. And looking prettier than any painted picture possibly could, were the flitches of bacon that hung from the hooks on the walls. The family had fed their piglet through the spring, summer and autumn. Now HE would feed THEM through the winter!

At last, for a few days at the festive season, they could relax, eat, drink and be merry. And I hope you can too! A very happy Christmas to you all.

69 January 1987 Field Names
NAMES CONJURE UP VISIONS OF THE PAST

If ever I have time to spare - which is very rare - one of my delights on a cold winter's evening is to relax in my favourite armchair, toast my toes in front of the crackling wood fire and browse through an old book. Or pore with pleasure over ancient maps and manuscripts, deeds, documents and details of life long ago.

It is amazing the amount of information on local lore that can be gleaned from such a simple subject as field and farm names. Take my own for instance. Until recently, on most larger scale maps my farm was called 'The Mill House', because succeeding generations of corn millers had lived here. When I moved in, nearly thirty years ago, I was

74

fortunate to get the name reverted to its original title, 'The Golden Cross', for until the 1880s it was the village pub!

Being so close to the church it shared in the social activities of the parish, especially at the Wakes. The field in front of my farmhouse is still called the 'Bear Hole' from the bear-baiting that took place upon it on festive occasions. Cockfights were staged on the field adjoining the church and many parishes have a 'Cockpit Field' to commemorate its former use. The hunting and

netting of the erratic twilight roding woodcock gave rise to the well-known names of 'Cocksmoss', 'Cockshutt' and their many variants.

Keepers bred rabbits in fenced warrens; only the youngsters were called 'rabbits'. Adults were called 'coneys', as the fur still is - hence the name of another field on my farm: 'Coney Greave', the rabbit warren!

'Horse Pastures' are very common. Nearby are two examples, 'Big Horse Field' and 'Little Horse Field'. Incidentally, the names do not relate to the size of the animal but to the size of the fields! Adjacent is 'Dobbins Croft' - the retirement paddock for old horses kept mainly to tread the sheaves at harvest.

Even older methods of cultivation are recalled in the 'Ox Pastures', in which the large white ox-daisies grow.

'Fox-holes' and 'Pheasants Covert' are frequently found and Brock the badger has left his mark on many a map in the 'Brock Hole' or 'Badger Wood'. Another animal appears in the form of 'Hare Hill', but did you know that 'Mawkins Land' means "where hares are seen"? 'Urchins Moor' suggests that hedgehogs were once more numerous than now, but rooks still regularly congregate on 'Crow Park'.

Lizards have long since left 'Askers Meadow' and within the last ten years have almost vanished from my garden and the churchyard too. Geese no longer breed on 'Goosemere' nor at 'Gosling Green', but they are still remembered in name. As are others with 'Adders Field', 'Ravens Marsh', 'Bucks Hill', 'Doe Field', 'Hawks Head' and 'Crakes Marsh' (corn crake).

Trees have given a location to 'Holly Bank', 'Broad Oak', 'Wicken Hall' (mountain ash), 'Maypole Meadow', 'Cherry Barrow', 'Crab Tree Moss', 'Plum Tree Plot', 'Hazel Wall' and the villages of 'Capesthorne' and 'Alderley', among many others.

Meanwhile, marl was extracted from the marl pits at 'Marl Heath', sand from the 'Sand-pits' and 'Sand-bank'. Whetstones were quarried from the 'Cutting Knife Field', and larger round ones from 'The Grindstones'.

The wind was utilised to separate the chaff from the grain at 'Winnowing Bank', and clay to make bricks was taken from 'Brickbank'. They were fired on the 'Brick-kiln Field', part of 'Brick-kiln Farm', with charcoal made in the nearby 'Colshaw Wood' (Charcoal Copse)!

From time immemorial, each area had a particular piece of land set aside for religious purposes. The trees and bushes around were cleared and sometimes a mound was erected. Villages formed around these sites often contain 'ley' in their names if a clearing and 'low' if a mound, as at Alderley, Bosley, Butley, Disley, Shrigley, Alcumlow, Brownlow and Wilmslow.

When Christianity arrived, churches were often built on these clearings or mounds. The land immediately surrounding was called 'God's acre', 'God's yard' or as we now call it the 'church yard'. These sites, chosen by dowsers, usually emitted a positive euphoric aura of happiness and well being, especially at certain times of the year.

Our ancestors, riddled with the rigours of superstition, set aside a similar plot of land for the use of the devil (often referred to as Jack). Again, dowsers chose the site, an opposite one which emitted a negative atmosphere of evil and depression from the earth's energy fields. These areas were left uncultivated and uncropped to allow the devil to amuse himself upon them and so not pester their crops or plague their animals. These sites have been handed down to us in the names 'No man's land' and in my own parish 'Jack's croft'; many other examples abound locally!

On several occasions in our history we have had a 'Dad's Army'. Laws compelled all able-bodied men to practise with their 'artillery' - bows and arrows - for at least two hours after divine service each Sunday. As the parish armour and armaments were usually stored in the church, the churchyard became their parade ground.

There they arrayed themselves and fired arrows at targets set at progressive intervals away - 'short butts', 'middle butts' and 'long butts', still found as field names around churches. The distance of the 'butt' was shorter than a 'shot' - the length of a furrow - 220 yards - a 'furlong'. Greater distances were marked by 'long shot' in the naming of fields.

The 'adlands' or 'headlands' was the space provided at the end of the field for the draught animals to turn their heads (and selves) around when working. These ends were often dug over with spades after the horses or the oxen had finished ploughing.

People frequently incorrectly connect the spade with field names like 'dig butts', 'dig field', 'dig hole' or 'dig lake'. In fact, 'dig' was the old name for domesticated ducks so they really mean 'duck field', 'duck hole' and 'duck lake'.

The prefix or suffix of 'carr' or 'flash' warns of fields liable to flooding, whilst 'sutch' and 'slough', 'mire' and 'moss', 'bog' and 'marsh' all denoted very wet and often dangerous ground.

Most villages had their 'hemp' and 'flax fields' showing the importance of those crops in the past. Hemp stems were retted and its fibres spun into rope or woven into coarse cloth - sail cloth and canvas. In former days hemp was used as a narcotic drug which induced halluci-nations, especially of flying, and was widely in demand by witches! Ordinary folk used hemp-seed for divination - to foretell the identity of a future lover and the date of their marriage. Its growth is now banned and its use forbidden, for its Greek name is *Cannabis*!

A field of flax in flower was said to ripple with the softness of the passing cumulus clouds and reflect the delicate blue of the sky above. Later the ripening stems stood upright like myriads of fine gossamer threads. When retted, the finished flax fibres hung like tresses of pale yellow hair - as the song says. Because its Latin name was *linum*, the fine fabric into which it was woven became LINEN!

The seed was also very important; from it was extracted an oil - linseed - which could be coated into wood as a preservative. Mixed with oxides and ochres it became paint; mixed with whiting it became putty. When boiled and ignited linseed made an extremely sticky glue - 'bird lime' - which was used to catch small birds and mice. In quantity, linseed oil was a purgative but in small amounts it soon put a lovely 'bloom' on to any animal regularly fed with it.

Freshly woven linen from the cottages was soaked then stretched out on frames in the fields to dry. Hooks passed through the selvedge to keep it taut and to stop it blowing away while the sun bleached the cloth white. This was called 'tentering'. However, in this state a careful eye had to be kept on the weather. If the wind got up it might rip or tear the cloth. If it rained the cloth might be damaged by uneven spotting.

Most of our villages had 'tenter' or 'tentry' fields, and when the linen was out the weavers were so anxious that they were said 'to be on tenterhooks'! From this expression also derives the name of any temporary shelter of stretched canvas - a tent!

I hope that you have enjoyed sharing with me some of the 'secrets' that lie behind the forgotten origins of the field names of our countryside.

70 February Fleas
BEWARE! THE BLACK ARMY IS GETTING READY TO MARCH

Beware! This is the time of year that they suddenly appear. Tradition says that the 'Black Army' arrives on March 1st. On that day all diligent housewives should arise early, close the windows and clean every inch of the house including cracks and doorsteps to be rid of them for the coming year!

These parasites have been the scourge of mankind since the beginning of time. They have been responsible for changes in our farming practice, our furniture and our habits. They have spread diseases that have killed millions of people - yet they have amused millions more with their aerobatic antics.

Few of us older folk can truthfully say we have never been affected by them. They have caused many a restless night and as a consequence are often quoted in everyday language. In this country alone they come in a 'Heinz' assortment of 57 varieties, many of which have left their mark on mankind in more ways than one.

What are they? FLEAS.

Female fleas lay a batch of several hundred eggs which reach maturity in six weeks. At this stage they have the ability to remain dormant for up to a year. If they are aroused by the vibrations of a suitable host they will emerge from their cocoons together and hop onto their unsuspecting host, thus causing a sudden plague.

Once a house became infested the remedies our ancestors recommended were to scatter wormwood, pennyroyal or fennel on the floors and sprinkle a concoction of the rue around. If the outbreak occurred in the summer, a handful of fleabane had to be burned in every room every day during the months of June, July and August. Its smoke was reputed to repel the rascals. A later alternative was to scrub the floorboards and furniture with a mixture of soda, soap and paraffin.

But these precautions were of little protection against the deadliest parasite of all - the flea that lived on the black rat. Introduced into this country from ships carrying cargo from the eastern Mediterranean, the rats rapidly spread inland from the ports. The bite from an infected flea - itself dying of the deadly baccili that had just killed the rat - transferred the fatal rodent disease to humans, whose skin erupted into black spots. Hence the name of the epidemic: The Black Death

About half the population of the old world and two million of the four million in this country perished in the three major outbreaks between 1348 and 1380AD. Just as rats abandon a sinking ship, so fleas desert a dying person and for the next 300 years they hopped from one host to another to spread what we now know as the bubonic plague.

Many historians believe that people invented a simple ditty to remind them of the dangers of the disease. It listed the symptoms, possible preventatives and the almost inevitable end result, contained in a rhyme which children still recite today:

"Ring a ring of roses" - the ring of rosy coloured swellings, the the onset of the plague

"A pocket full of posies" - aromatic herbs and protective pomanders that people carried to sniff for protection when confronted with infection

"Atishoo, atishoo" - the feverish sneezing,

and the final phrase, "All fall down" - DEAD.

This is one of the reasons we still say, "Bless you" when anyone sneezes - in the hope of divine protection against the plague.

So many country people perished that the previous labour-intensive cultivation of corn crops gave way to the growing of grass and the grazing of sheep, which required relatively few shepherds. Wool became our 'staple' industry.

The human flea, *pulex ritans,* also frequents foxes, pigs and badgers. It is compressed from side to side to enable it to scramble through hair, fur and feathers. Its backward pointing spines make it difficult to dislodge.

Feathers were a favourite place for fleas to infest. And because feather beds were once a symbol of affluence they resulted in many disturbed dreams. For during the night the fleas would leave their nests and crawl out. If sufficient fleas feasted, the lethargic victim would voice his feelings next morning by proclaiming, "I feel lousy!" And from drunkards who collapsed on the floor arose another saying, "He who sleeps with the dogs shall rise with the fleas!"

Mattresses, bolsters, pillows and cushions that had become colonised (by fleas) were sterilised in the communal bake-ovens - after the weekly rations had been baked!

Partial respite arrived when a close-woven stout cloth was invented. This enclosed the mattress and prevented the access of fleas and ticks. As a result, it was called ticking.

Victorian chambermaids regularly spent half an hour searching the sheets when making the beds. They crushed any errant fleas between their thumbnails to ensure a more restful night for their employers!

Stuffed chairs and sofas were such a source of infestation that upholsterers were nicknamed bug-hunters; and one of the reasons behind the Victorian vogue for the cane chair was to reduce the possible breeding grounds of the flea.

An Elizabethan flea catcher

In the marketplace on a weekday or in church on a Sunday it was a familiar sight to see mothers utilising their spare time to advantage by going through their children's hair removing any lice and their eggs. This trivial occupation was called 'nit-picking' and has since come to mean "finding fault in a petty manner".

Monks and Catholic clergymen had a 'tonsure' haircut - leaving a corona of hair that represented the 'crown of thorns', but its practical purpose was to reduce the area available to vermin. The serviceman's 'short back and sides' was introduced for the same reason!

Around the mid and late 1700s the 'Madame Pompadour' type of high hair-dos were fashionable but expensive to create. They were therefore made to last as long as possible, with the inevitable result that they became infected. To combat the discomfort, ladies of leisure carried a knitting needle to scratch their heads and relieve the irritation without disturbing their 'beehive' hair arrangement. Perhaps it should have been called a 'NIT'ting needle'!

That same century a famous Scottish poet had his attention diverted from higher thoughts when he sat in church behind a very prim and proper lady. She had a flea crawling around her bonnet. It caused him to pen the immortal lines, "Oh wad some power the giftie gie us, to see ourself as ithers see us." The poet: Robert Burns (1759 - 1796).

A flea can jump a distance of a foot (30 cm) to reach another host or to avoid capture. In comparison, size for size, that means YOU and I could clear St. Paul's Cathedral with ease - and cover the 200 metre race in a single bound!

Because of their agility, fleas became the centre of curiosity when travelling showmen paraded their 'flea circus' at fairs and seaside resorts. Some of the tiny insects were harnessed to chariots, others walked tight ropes, hopped through hoops, lifted loads, climbed ladders or overcame obstacles. Between performances they were fed and housed in small containers strapped to the 'ringmaster's' wrists. Old fleas that had outlived their usefulness were given a new lease of life by being discreetly released among the gullible audience. It was one way of assuring that the performances always came up to scratch!

When a flea bites it injects some saliva to stop the blood clotting. It is our allergic reaction to this that raises the lump and causes the area to itch. Scientists have recently discovered a new use for this saliva - as an anti-coagulant on minute blood vessels when performing micro-surgery. Fortunately for the surgeons, larger quantities can be obtained more readily from leeches and vampire bats!

Fleas ingest more blood than they can digest, with the inevitable result that they leave their characteristic 'pock' marks on clothing and bed linen.

Fortunately, recent improvements in hygiene, new chemical deterrents and the frequent use of the vacuum cleaner have rendered flea-bites uncommon for the majority of us. Yet once we all had to bear our burdens - even the fleas themselves. For as the poem says,

Big fleas have little fleas,
Upon their backs to bite 'em
And little fleas have lesser fleas,
And so ad infinitum!

71 March Mad as March Hares
SPRING FEVER GRIPS MAD MARCH HARES

As mad as a March hare? Although hares mate and breed for much of the year, it is because these normally intelligent and timorous creatures suddenly change their habits that they have become part of our legendary mythology. For this is the 'rutting' season, when they discard the solitary survival instincts that they have exhibited over the previous eleven months and congregate for a display which can only be explained as a surge of 'spring fever' - an annual exhibition of their amorous intentions.

The male 'Jacks', as they are called, stand erect on their strong hind legs. They box and bite, paw and kick, leap and dodge the blows from one another, in a battle for

dominance over the harem. Patches of fur fly and flesh is torn in the tumult. It is a sign of their endurance that these contests can last a day or more.

Naturalists claim that the female 'Jills' also join in on occasions or scamper and chase one another around the combatants. They have also been known to sit in a circle contemplating the outcome in a similar way to rooks when they are 'holding court'. The eventual victor, having temporarily gained the upper hand, rolls over on to his back, wriggles and then turns his affections to the females. During the next few days he will mate with several of them, whilst they in turn may mate with other males.

The hare possesses the rare capability of carrying young of two different ages in her womb. An old Norfolk saying incorrectly states, "A mare and a hare go a year!" The gestation of the mare is eleven months but the hare requires 42 to 50 days, depending on the species, before she gives birth to two or three leverets, as the young are called. They are born, fully furred and with their eyes wide open, into a shallow depression called a 'form' or 'mews', somewhere in the middle of a big field.

Soon they are separated and taken to their own 'form', sheltered in the hollow between the plough furrows or hidden in bunches of grass. The doe visits them regularly to suckle. Between times the leverets lie motionless, relying on their excellent camouflage for protection against predators - buck rabbits, foxes, stoats, hawks and carrion crows.

A few hares are acceptable but a quantity (a down of hares) can be an expensive nuisance. Large patches of winter corn, eaten from the centres of the fields, mean a loss of income of two sacks of corn per hare! Although, in its favour, rooks seldom steal the seed corn where hares are plentiful. So stuffed hares were once widely used as scarecrows, which may explain why the nickname for them both is a 'mawkin'.

Hares also have a sweet tooth. They will nibble yard after yard along row after row of mangolds, swedes and sugar beet. They leave the leaves attached by a thin thread of stem which at best produces a deformed root and at worst wilts away - again, a deficit of two tons an acre a hare!

On grassland ten hares will eat as much as one sheep!

In the past the 'February tenants shoot' on this estate often yielded a bag of over 100 hares. Individual hares can be caught by an ingenious method of 'calling' which imitates their cry of alarm. It is produced by sucking air through moistened lips or off the back of the hand. On most occasions when I have used it the hare has come hopping inquisitively towards me, its black-tipped ears erect, certainly within shooting distance.

Children learn another method at play, not realising its origin. A strong blade of grass (cocksfoot type) is clamped taut between the upright thumbs. When air is blown through it gives a piercing note that can be varied in intensity by opening and closing the cupped hands behind. Special 'hare callers' or 'pipes' could also be purchased from gunshops.

By any of these methods, poachers would entice hares within range of their unleashed greyhounds. They were specially trained to nose between the hare's back legs and topple it head over heels to prevent it swerving away. Whippets, being faster on the turn, when the hare suddenly twisted, chased from the side!

The amazing agility of the hare demanded a good dog to catch it. With their longer back legs they can run uphill faster than down and reach a speed of 40 mph. They can leap over a seven foot wall, stop and/or reverse direction instantaneously and are excellent swimmers!

During 'coursing' the bucks tend to run in a straight line, the does in a circle. The

'chase' lasts anything from a few seconds to two minutes before the hare is snapped up or has eluded its pursuers. But a hunt with hounds could take up to two hours and cover several miles before the exhausted hare was finally cornered by the pack, often within a few feet of where it was lifted!

St. Moncella became the patron saint of hares when one escaped by hiding beneath her skirt whilst she was praying and he was being 'hounded'.

A hare's curiosity can also be the cause of its downfall, as in another ancient method of capture. One person waved a rag a short distance in front of the squatting hare whilst another moved downwind and came up stealthily behind. The hare's attention was so focussed upon the unusual antics in front it failed to see the predator behind!

Hares are not infested with vermin; they groom themselves meticulously, being specially equipped for doing so by a brush on each foot! Their fur makes a very high quality felt and commanded a good price for making hats. Their skins were used to bind books. People also believed they assumed the abilities of the animal if they wore its skin as a coat. Thus hare skins gave them the power of extreme endurance! Pelts of inferior quality were made into mats. Still, as Mrs Beeton is often misquoted as saying, "First - catch your hare!"

Many country people will not eat hare meat; some say they are tough, taste strong, are hard to digest, messy with blood and induce bad dreams of incubus. This may be correct in an elderly adult animal of some four or five years but I have always found leverets quite a luxury. Young hares were traditionally sacrificed to celebrate a birth and the flesh was eaten joyfully.

But there were many deep reasons for disliking the meat of a hare. Eating a timid and melancholy animal might make you feel the same. Witches could turn into hares at will so you might be eating human flesh in disguise and therefore inadvertently be a cannibal! - although it was widely supposed that a hare-witch could only be killed with a silver bullet, even more potent if made from a silver coin with a cross upon it. Should a pregnant woman have a hare cross her path, the only way to avoid her child being born with a 'hare lip was to immediately tear her petticoat.

From the beginning of civilisation the hare has received world-wide recognition as a creature of mystery and magic. It is depicted in ancient cave paintings. Noah used the hare's front right foot to plug a leak in the ark; since then it has been the symbol of good luck, also recently transferred to the rabbit!

The Hebrews thought the hare to be an hermaphrodite because of its unusual sexual organs, sometimes male, sometimes female. Some suggested it changed its sex on a monthly or yearly cycle and that even the males could bear young. Ancient Greek wedding rings had the emblem of a hare upon them as a symbol of love and fertility.

The Egyptians kept hares in special preserves and used them in their hieroglyphics for a word meaning 'existence' - 'to be' - (or not 'to be' - that is the question). China has the year of the hare and believes it is a hare, not a man, in the moon! The American Indians and nomadic tribes the world over believed in the 'great hare' who was a teacher and kept everyone in a great bag until he had made the world fit for them to live in again.

Boadicea used a hare as an omen and consequently conquered her enemies.

Both the hare and the cat were familiars to the 'White Goddess'.

The hare was an attendant spirit that carried the candles for Oestre the Goddess of the Dawn, the Spring and the beginning of the year, formerly celebrated on March 25th when people shouted "Hare, hare, hare." Now at the beginning of every moonth (month) people say, "Rabbits, rabbits, rabbits!"

The hare was once a symbol of Easter and it was originally the hare who hid the Easter eggs around the garden. Like the egg, the hare symbolised rebirth and the resurrection. With the arrival of Christianity the attributes of the pagan hare were slowly replaced by the rabbit - the Easter Bunny!

With all these inheritances in its ancestry, is it any wonder that this curious creature goes mad in March!

72 April Seeds
THE SECRETS OF MOTHER NATURE'S OWN COMPUTERS

In this modern age you may marvel at the wonders of electronic wizardry, the minuteness of the complex circuitry of the silicon chip or be amazed by the performance of programmed computers.

But have you ever realised that Mother Nature has been busily programming her way ahead in a parallel manner for thousands of centuries already?

Condensing a whole host of information into an extremely small space is nothing new to nature, for safely stored in every seed is a series of cells that contain a computer-like programme, packed with all the complex instructions that the seed will ever need in order to grow to maturity and produce a similar seed of its own! Yet because it is such a commonplace occurrence we tend to take it for granted. Few ever bother to think of the miraculous mechanism that lies behind it.

To protect the seed from disease, damage or drying out it is usually housed in a hardened skin. Inside are sufficient nutrients to enable it to establish a root system and so gain a start in life. Also locked away somewhere in that structure, seldom bigger than a pinhead and often smaller than a pin prick, is a central source of information just waiting to be tapped - waiting until the correct conditions for growth appear, when the warmth and solar energy from the sun combine with moisture from rain or floods to trigger the seed's own in-built computer and set its germination programme in motion.

Already programmed into the process are the details of how high the plant is to grow, the size, shape and position of its leaves, the type and colour of its flowers, the kind of seedcase and the number of seeds to be produced!

Human computer codes can be broken into and the information interpreted and used by others, but a seed holds its secrets until it comes to fruition; the information held inside the humble seed is not available to mere mortals!

An experienced gardener can tell at a glance what type of seed it is by its shape, size and colour, and by knowledge gained over the years can picture the type of plant it is likely to produce. But unless the seed has been specifically separated, the colour of the flower of say, a sweet pea, wallflower or pansy, cannot be foretold by examining the seed! It has to be grown. And that's another mystery.

As soon as the plant starts to grow the seed dies. Where has that programme of information been transferred to in the undeveloped seedling? Even at this stage, it is not possible to predict the colour of the final flower! It is not until the bud emerges and the petals open that we are let into the secret that the seed has known all along!

After the flower has been visited by the bees and the seeds set, it is still not always possible to know the colour of the next generation of flowers unless the plant has been isolated and pollinated from a known source. Fortunately, in most plants, like produces like and with that little bit of expertise we have learned that a small round black seed that produces a turnip in its first year will yield yellow flowers and a further supply of similar turnip seed in the second season.

In contrast, the tiny black seed of a poppy will shoot up, flower and seed in the same season and from its covered conical cup the wind will shake its ripened seeds onto the ground all around.

And that's another of the wonders of seeds; how they are programmed in advance to escape from the parent plant in such ingenious ways. When ripened, the dandelion produces its famous 'clock' cluster of seeds, until the wind bears each one 'up, up and away', suspended beneath a 'pappus' parachute. Thistle-down also drifts across my pastures to infest future grazing unless I remember to cut the thistles down first! Rosebay willowherb and ragwort do the same with such success that during the wartime blitzes even the city centre bomb sites were quickly colonised with their pretty pink and yellow blooms.

Other plants are programmed to encase their seeds inside a fleshy berry. Birds eat the berry, digest the flesh for food and pass the protected seed out with their droppings - onto a fresh site. In this way the mistlethrush spreads the mistletoe and blackbirds and thrushes the raspberry, elderberry and blackcurrants.

Any farmer who has applied untreated sewage sludge to his land has probably been puzzled by the large number of perplexing plants that suddenly appear. They are in fact tomato seedlings that have not been broken down by our stomach juices! We also transfer seeds in the tread of our car tyres and on our boots and shoes, whilst wildfowl can carry seeds over continents in the mud that clings to their webbed feet!

Cleavers, sticky burrs and goosegrass are programmed to produce hooks which will hang onto any passing animal, transporting the seed until it drops off, gets dislodged or receives the 'brush-off'!

Gorse and broom 'pop' the peas from their pods on hot sunny days. They shoot some considerable distance - as anyone passing a bush at the time will soon discover. The common vetch has developed an even more devious device. Built into its programme is the command that, as the seed pod bursts, the two half-cases immediately spring into a spiral, catapulting the seeds far away from the parent plant to found another colony.

Some tall trees such as sycamore, ash and lime are programmed to equip their seeds with propellers. This slows down their descent and enables the breeze to blow them further away from the tree, giving them a greater chance of survival.

Seeds are often unwittingly sown by animals. Squirrels, rats and mice will hoard acorns and then forget where they are stored. Occasionally some may grow. Children of my day and age made 'pop' guns from hollow elderberry stems. With these we would shoot our 'acorn' projectiles many yards in defence of our battlegrounds. In so doing, I may have given some tiny acorn an unintentional start in life; even now it may be maturing into a mighty oak!

Nearly all seeds have another vital safety factor programmed into their system for survival. They will not start to germinate until the conditions are correct. Many varieties can exist for hundreds of years in the soil. During the last war I remember pastures that had never been ploughed in living memory. They produced a crop of arable weeds in the first season. One weed was 'fat hen', once grown as a vegetable by our ancestors. It is known for a fact that wild raspberry pips eaten by Roman soldiers 1700 years ago will still germinate. But I cannot confirm the stories that corn seeds taken from the tombs of Egyptian mummies have germinated four thousand years later. Perhaps that story needs to be taken with a 'grain' of salt!

Wild oats are weeds that have spread so rapidly of late that they have become a menace. They are programmed with two extra secrets for survival: firstly, a wax coating which stops them absorbing sprays that kill most other plants and secondly, they mature before the cereal crop in which they grow. These two factors make them extremely difficult to eradicate.

In some seasons my garden has hundreds of tiny laburnums fighting for survival; other years there are none. It seems to depend on the severity of the winter. The seeds need to be exposed to **very** hard frosts before they will consider growing.

The toughness of the seed's protective skin can cause problems to gardeners. Lupins have a terrible germination record unless the seed is first nicked with a knife. Parsley also shoots so slowly that it is said to "return to the devil nine times before it will come up for you." For this reason it is traditionally sown on Good Friday - when the devil has no jurisdiction over the soil - and boiling water is poured over the planted seed to "scald the devil."

"Where parsley thrives the 'Old Grey Mare' is the better horse!" In other words, the wife wears the trousers! Also, whilst boy babies are grown under the gooseberry bush, girls are produced in the parsley patch (it's an aphrodisiac)!

The number of seeds the plant is to produce is also programmed into the seed. The lower the survival rate, the greater the number of seeds that are required. A poppy will produce 50,000, a thistle about half that number and most weeds several thousand! Is it any wonder that "One year's seeding means seven years weeding."

Yes, seeds are certainly one of Mother Nature's many miracles; the secrets of survival are programmed into every seed sown - Nature's natural computers.

73 May Nests
ANYTHING GOES, IN THE BIRDS' NESTING SEASON

In my mind's eye I can picture it now. Safely stored out of harm's way in the farmhouse attic of my childhood was a large brown wooden box with a glass lid and drawers underneath. I wasn't allowed to touch it, for inside, neatly labelled and carefully laid on a cotton wool lining, was my father's impressive display of dozens of different birds' eggs.

When I was a lad it was a common and exciting springtime hobby to search for the nests of wild birds. There was always the thrill of finding a different species to add to the collection.

It was the unwritten rule that only one egg was ever taken from a nest. Before display the contents had to be emptied. To do this, both ends of the egg were pricked with a pin and the liquid yolk and white blown out. Sometimes there was a developing chick inside. Then the alternative method was to puncture one end only and lay the egg beside an active ants' nest. They would clear the contents in a matter of hours!

Surplus specimens were swapped at school from lined tobacco tins. There were a great many more birds about in those days. A thick thorn hedge would have a nest every twenty or thirty yards - about eighty to the mile. Since I biked eight and a half miles home from school it was no wonder I was often late for tea or had a rent in my regulation grey short trousers caused from climbing the many ivy-clad and hollow trees en route.

My exploits made me appreciate the instinctive intricacy of the construction of the nests themselves. A base of wispy twigs, interwoven with stout grasses, often precariously perched in the fork of a branch yet seldom dislodged by wind or weather. Inside the cup-shaped container was a lining of mud, finer grasses, soft moss, feathers, hair or wool, which, when you think about it, affords a draught-proof protective cradle for the eggs and chicks inside.

By comparison, ground-nesting birds are distinctly lazy. They often only scrape a hollow depression in the earth which they line with grass.

I spotted a new partridge nest in a hedge bank last week with four of a possible clutch of ten to twenty eggs already laid. When she has completed her clutch, she will start incubating them so that they all emerge together - 24 days later.

On my previous farm lapwings - peewits - were a problem. They nested in the sugar beet drills and corn rows. The parent bird would try to lure you away from her nest by feigning a broken wing and crying pitifully or dive bomb and attack if you approached too close. The waggoner and I had a seasonal competition to see who could discover the most nests. On finding one, a stick was stuck upright nearby so that the eggs would not get smashed when we were horse-hoeing, harrowing or rolling the field.

Much more difficult to detect was the skylark. She laid her four or five mottled earth-brown eggs in the hollow imprint left by a cow's hoof. These cunning little creatures ran several yards from the nest after being disturbed before soaring into the sky above, singing. However, with a little patience and a thorough search of the area, another stick would mark yet another site to be protected.

Each year tiny wrens build somewhere around the farmyard. The male usually constructs several ball-shaped nests. The favoured female chooses one and finishes it off to her liking. Frequently they are found near to the ground and within easy reach of our cats, which have to be shut up as soon as the fledglings are ready to fly. This year they have chosen a site just underneath our bedroom window. I can just imagine in a few days' time my wife and I will be awakened, not by our alarm clock, but by the shrill staccato alarm of our wrens!

During the winter we feed our garden birds with offcuts of fat, inverted coconuts and bags of peanuts, all strung out along the washing line. To compensate us, they have since left a deposit on my wife's washing when hung out to dry - we will have to change their feeding place in future! However, the blue tits are looking into the nesting box and a couple of holes in the apple tree. The long-tailed tits will probably build their beautiful domed bottle-shaped nest of moss, lichen and cobwebs, lined with silky bantam feathers, at their usual site, in the gorse bushes across the river. There they will raise their dozen or so chicks.

Our ancient apple tree has added yet another success to its list this year. For on a low bough a mistle-thrush (storm cock) has constructed its nest. As a foundation it has used the coiled and knotted rope of my granddaughter's garden swing! And as an added attraction its twigs and grasses are interwoven with white ribbon collected from churchyard wreaths - just over the fence! As soon as the swing is used, four gaping mouths appear over the rim of the nest, much to the alarm of the anxious parents!

The churchyard and its surrounding fence also provided the materials for another happy event. Strands of cowhair collected from the barbed wire, beakfuls of moss and lichen from the gravestones and a generous sprinkling of confetti from a wedding party made a delightfully different happy home for a chaffinch in one of the churchyard's curious 'umbrella' shaped trees.

A few years ago a religious robin discovered a broken pane in one of the latticed windows of the church and built its nest behind a massive oak roof truss. It wasn't until the fledglings flew around inside that the nest was discovered. By a strange coincidence, that autumn one of our lady choristers died. She loved robins. During her funeral a robin flew in, landed on her coffin and then flew out again - how's that for appreciation?

A lone ash tree in one of my further fields has a very interesting history connected to a single nesting site. Many years ago I spotted a small cavity where a branch had fallen from the trunk - tits were using the hole. The next occupants were woodpeckers. Starlings followed and in recent years it has been utilised by jackdaws, doves, kestrels and tawny owls - seven different species in all.

An oak tree blew down on the riverbank opposite our living room window; its roots left a large hollow. A kingfisher burrowed its slightly upward sloping tunnel a yard or so into the sandy soil. We watched it on many occasions and sometimes saw it perched motionless on a low branch by the bridge. At the end of the season my son put his arm into the hole to remove the nest. What he found was a handful of small, smelly fish bones.

At the moment three young mallard drakes are vying for the attention of a duck down by the stream. If the pattern of past years is repeated, her nest will either be in the shelter of the thick holly bush or in the rough patch of reeds and nettles under the alder tree.

Because coots and waterhens have nested just above the water this year, country people say a dry spring is in the offing. When they nest high above the water it denotes a wet spell. But grebes don't have to predict the weather, they nest on a floating raft anchored to the reeds. Their nest rises and falls with the water level.

Starlings often nest in downspouts and frequently get flushed out when it rains. One that caused quite a commotion nested in our chimney pot. When we lit the fire it smoked both them and us out!

Each year brings a fresh crop of unusual nesting sites, like the rook who wished to know which way the wind was blowing and nested on the church weather vane. A robin reached the dizzy heights when it chose to rear its young on top of a working merry-go-round. Exhibited in Chester Museum is a wren's nest inside the carcase of a sparrowhawk that had been hung on a gamekeeper's gibbet! Many records exist of felons who after death were 'hung in chains' - until the birds of the air nested in the bones!

Yet nature, too, can wreak its revenge, as in the case of the sparrow that took over a house martin's nest before completion. The martins continued building, sealed up the entrance and completely entombed the sparrow in retaliation!

Free range hens often raise their brood in a clump of nettles and proudly bring their chicks home to the farmyard for inspection when hatched. But on our former farm there was one hen laying away somewhere and we just couldn't find her nest. Her comb was red, she cackled and clucked, and she seemed to be laying daily. Eventually we discovered her nest, under the thorn hedge right beside the pavement - but there was only one egg in it. It took us another couple of days to solve the mystery of the missing eggs.

We farmed on the outskirts of a small market town and each afternoon a respectable middle-aged lady walked her dog along the pavement, stopped at the nest, stooped down and popped an egg into her bag. If we confronted her she was the sort that might well cause trouble in future. We couldn't fill an egg with mustard, as we did when our own hens or magpies were pinching and eating them. Then we had an idea.

Under a fowl pen were some addled eggs - really rotten and brown with age!! We polished a couple up with some Vim until they shone like new. Next day after dinner we took the genuine new-laid egg from the nest and replaced it with the two addled eggs. She fell for the bait - by teatime the two eggs had disappeared and as far as I can recollect so too did the lady and her dog. For she never walked past our farm again! I bet her kitchen smelled for days afterwards - rotten eggs, hydrogen sulphide, and memories of stink bombs at school!

Which brings me back to thinking about that large brown box with its glass lid. I've often wondered what happened to my father's egg collection. Oh, and by the way - disturbing birds' eggs is illegal nowadays so I usually take them with a camera instead!!!

74 June Cows' Horns
WHERE HAVE ALL THE COWS' HORNS GONE?

One of the many changes that have taken place during my thirty years of farming here, is that cows no longer have HORNS.

Horns used to be an important identifying feature of the animal. Ayrshires were equipped with a vicious-looking, upward curving, pointed pair. Shorthorns, as their name suggests, were short and stubby. Many a cow had a crumpled horn, disfigured by being dislodged or damaged during its formative months - whilst still a 'greenhorn'. Scottish Longhorns were beautifully marked and tapered, and a pair frequently decorated a

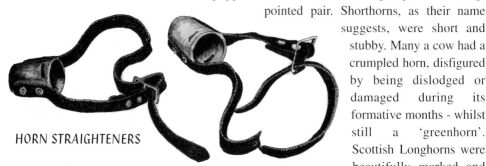

HORN STRAIGHTENERS

Used to correct any defect in the curve of horns for show cattle, especially Ayrshires.

doorway or hung over the mantlepiece mirror in farmhouses and inns of yesteryear.

The reason that horns are not seen today except on 'special breed farms' is that they are dangerous. They can cause a lot of damage both to workers and to other cows. In fights for dominance in the herd horned cows gored each other. They caused gashes which became infected by flies and bruised udders that flared into mastitis. Cows without horns are much less aggressive and therefore easier to manage in the crowded conditions and confined spaces of the collecting yards required by the large herds of today.

It was about 25 years ago that we farmers went through a phase of removing horns from all our adult animals - including in my case my bull! It was often a bloody business but fortunately it only had to be done once. The improvement in the temperament of both the cows and myself was immediately apparent! From then on all calves had their horn buds removed before they developed.

Yet horns were a valuable animal by-product and provided several important items to our heritage.

For the first three years of growth horns are smooth, then they develop ridges according to the age of the animal. They consist of two parts, a tough exterior called a horn and a softer, spongy, fat-filled but still horny interior called a 'flint'. This core fits inside the horn like a finger fits a glove and was removed by boiling. The resultant fat was widely used as the basic ingredient in the soap industry. The residual sponge went to the bone mills to be ground into 'hoof and horn' meal.

To make flat articles from horn the tip was removed - this was often carved into a thimble - the horn was cut down one side, steamed or baked, then flattened under pressure. Lengths were cut and the layers separated to the required thickness with a rough knife. To make a comb, 12 teeth were traditionally cut in by hand. The finished shape was scrubbed with coarse salt which produced the shine and brought out the colour.

An early use for the thin transparent slivers was to fill in the spaces between latticed laths to make a window. This was soon superseded by glass and lead. In a similar way, slivers of horn, held in place by a tin surround, protected candles from wind and draught. When transportable they were called 'lant-horns'. Later, when the horn was replaced by glass, which allowed more light through, the name changed to 'lanterns'.

Children learned their alphabet, Roman numerals and the Lord's Prayer from 'horn-books'. They were written on a single sheet of paper or parchment, stuck to a thin wooden backboard about 9in x 6in with a carrying handle and covered with a layer of transparent horn for protection. A hole in the handle allowed it to be tied to the child's girdle for keeping. Pictured before and after each of the three written items was a Maltese Cross - 'Christ's Cross' - 'Chris Cross' - or, as we now say, 'criss-cross'!

A modern use for the thicker flat section is as a 'horn knife' and many a desk drawer contains one for opening envelopes. The handle is often decoratively carved to add to its appeal.

Whole horns were used to pour drenches of medicine down animals' throats. If the tip was removed the horn was transformed into a funnel.

Countrymen carried horns at harvest which contained a mixture of grease and sand. This they smeared onto their square oaken sticks to convert them into sanding sticks to sharpen their sickles and scythes.

For those of us with shrunken shoes or swollen feet, half a horn when polished makes an excellent 'shoe-horn'. And to aid the housewife two sturdy spoons could be cut from a single horn. They were, and still are, ideal for stirring jams and other boiling liquids as they are light in weight, do not conduct heat, bend, break, warp or become brittle. They do not absorb flavours nor lose their surface and will last a lifetime. These qualities also made horn an ideal material for measuring scoops for chemists and grocers, and (who knows?) you may even have one hidden in your tea caddy at this moment!

Drinking beakers were cut from lengths of round horn. A flattened horn disc was 'sprung' into a circular groove a little way up from the bottom giving it a waterproof joint. Because they were cheap to make, easy to keep clean and almost indestructible, they were widely used in the home, especially by children, and being light were carried into the fields for use by the workers. For these reasons, too, the medical professions, especially in the Forces, used small transparent horn beakers as measures in the Crimean and First World Wars.

Soldiers of old carried muskets. They required gunpowder, which, if it got wet, was useless. So to "keep their powder dry" it was stored in horns with tight-fitting lids.

Engraved and embossed with silver, they fetch high prices at auction nowadays as 'powder horns'.

The ageing ailment of failing eyesight was improved by wearing horn-rimmed spectacles, whilst the hard of hearing used a horn as an ear-trumpet. Trumpet horns were used before bells to summon people to church on Saints' Days and Sundays and also to warn of invasion - by the Vikings.

Ancient charter horns that pre-date written records can still be seen in some cathedrals, museums or town halls. The transfer of property or tracts of land was 'drunk to' by all present and the new occupier kept the horn as proof of ownership.

Horns were also blown to summon parishioners to the tything and commoners to their rights. In some areas they sounded every evening at dusk to guide travellers across trackless wastes and through almost impenetrable forests. They enforced the curfew at 9pm - a custom continued to this day at Ripon. There the 'Wakeman' blew from the four corners of the market square to signal the start of his night watch, to protect the citizens from robbery and violence until daybreak. He also carried a horn to mark the hours of the night and to sound any alarm.

Drenching horn, funnel, ear trumpet - or just for blowing, as little boy blue did

Huntsmen kept their hounds in check with them, and coaches announced their arrival by the post-horn. Farmworkers used them to call their animals, as in the nursery rhyme "Little Boy Blue, come blow on your horn, the sheep's in the meadow, the cow's in the corn."

On a lighter note, waits sang to them, sailors danced to them, and they were worn at a ceremony of initiation by shepherds who had 'come of age'.

In many early religions the bull was sacred; its horns were the symbol of power, might and virility, and projected from each corner of their altars. It was on the 'horns of the altar' that Roman oaths were sworn and in Biblical days criminals were safe from prosecution as long as they grasped them. The Christian church continued this right of 'sanctuary' and extended it to 40 days but it was widely abused. To counteract this, if anyone committed a serious offence the parishioners would raise a 'hue and cry' - blow their horns, yell and shout, to warn those who lived near the church to barricade the doors and prevent the offender gaining access to the 'sanctuary'. If the criminal was caught, convicted and outlawed his sentence was pronounced by three blasts on a horn.

A few years ago I was on the 'horns of a dilemma' myself, for when I wished to get my cows into calf I could no longer "take the bull by the horns". Instead I now have to rely on the services of the artificial inseminator - the A.I. man. As soon as he arrives in my farmyard he announces his presence by blowing his HORN! I think there must be a moral in that somewhere!

75 July Country 'Complaints'
EVERYDAY PERILS THAT AFFLICT 'HEALTHY' COUNTRY FOLK

Some people rant and rave about the healthiness of living in the countryside. Others are equally adamant that rural life is not all it's cracked up to be and they are full of "complaints".

At this time of the year, and especially during the glorious hot fortnight we have just had, swollen eyes, runny noses and sneezing sessions have been the typical symptoms of hay fever sufferers. Every day millions of tiny particles of pollen are released from flowering trees, plants and grasses. From cottage gardens, roadside verges, hedge banks and hayfields they are wafted away with the wind to irritate and inflame the sensitive membranes of vulnerable victims, making their lives a misery. Their best protection is to stay indoors with windows closed and curtains drawn and pray for wet weather to wash the pollen grains harmlessly to the ground.

But wet weather brings its problems too! On damp, dead and decaying matter grow moulds and mildew that give off spores which when inhaled can drastically damage the lining of the lungs in animals and man. These moulds are often found around the edges of silage clamps, corn silos and feeding troughs and are particularly nasty in damp hay. The grey dustiness given off causes a complaint commonly known by country people as 'farmer's lung'.

This 'shortage of breath' used to be very noticeable among the teams of men who toured the farms threshing corn stacks. Sometimes the stacks were badly thatched, frequently damp and always dusty. Protective face masks were unheard of and any 'cissy' who covered his nose and mouth with a handkerchief was laughed to scorn by all and sundry.

The serious consequences of mouldy hay and grain weren't confined to those who inhaled its dust but also to the animals that ate it. Under certain conditions the animal lost its offspring part-way through its pregnancy.

An even deadlier and more dreaded disease which was once rampant in livestock areas was *brucella abortus*. It was so contagious that it could create a 'storm' in a herd of cattle and nearly every cow would cast its calf before its time. This heralded financial disaster for the farmer. Not only was the premature calf a 'dead' loss but the poor cow produced no extra milk and was difficult to get back into calf. It happened to me soon after I started farming; twenty-three out of my twenty-five cows aborted in a single season! But like many other farmers in my area, I had to weather the 'storm'; there was no compensation in those days.

Improved vaccines gradually reduced the severity of the outbreaks and later all reactors were automatically slaughtered. Disastrous as it was for the farmer, the outbreaks of abortion often spread to the village people beyond. The bacilli could and would kill babies as easily as calves and was once a frequent cause of miscarriage in country families.

Another form the bacteria took was called 'undulant fever'. Its symptoms were often confused with malaria; monthly phases of sweating, trembling, lethargy and depression, especially among farmers, their workers, vets, slaughterers and butchers - anyone who handled contaminated carcasses.

Another infection common to animals and humans alike was 'consumption' or 'tuberculosis'. Suggested aids (for people) were smelling hot tar, sniffing cow's and sheep's breath early in the morning, complete rest or removal to a sanatorium, often surrounded by pine trees whose fragrance was thought to help. One of the first cows I ever owned caught tuberculosis and wasted away to skin and bones.

A story my dad used to delight to tell was of the half-witted country lad who arrived at the farm with the family milk can to be filled. He was told, "Sorry, but there's no milk for you today, me boy; the cow's got tuberculosis." The lad went home crying with his empty can and told his mother, "Farmer says there's no milk today because the cow's got two-little-hosses."

It was long suspected that milk was one of the main culprits in spreading tuberculosis and brucellosis. The old advice was to boil all suspected milk before drinking. This advice was confirmed by Louis Pasteur, the famous French chemist and scientist. The process of heating milk was later undertaken by the dairies and carries his name to this day: pasteurisation. Nowadays, the M.M.B. central laboratory at Harrogate tests samples of milk from almost every herd in the country every week to ensure that the daily delivery on your doorstep is free from any such harmful impurities.

Unsightly, bald, often round, patches of scaly skin, that itch as though a worm is burrowing beneath, gave the name to a fungal infection known as 'ringworm'. Some winters all my young stock catch it - others none. Cod liver oil, sunlight and spring grass soon seem to kill it off. It can be easily caught by touching where the animals have rubbed. However, it usually only appears badly once in each lifetime as both animals and ourselves appear to build up an immunity against it.

I once caught an infectious and irritating rash called erysipelas from my saddleback sows. It is also called diamonds from the shape of the streptococcus sores.

When I was young, I could never understand why I sometimes woke up wheezing in the early hours of the morning, especially Sunday. What I didn't know until years later was that it was asthma. Every Saturday I earned extra pocket money by cleaning the poultry manure from the dropping boards of the hen houses. I received a penny a pen - a shilling for half a day's work! I lived a life of luxury - except in the early hours of Sunday morning!

When I was called up into the Forces my wheeziness left me. It only returned when I went home on leave. Then I discovered why. In the R.E.M.E. I slept on a donkey's breakfast - a mattress of three straw 'biscuits' - at home I was featherbedded! I was allergic to feathers!

Gardeners often find they come up in a rash when working with certain flowers. Some people cannot bear to have a cat or dog around the house because of the problems they cause, whilst others are allergic to work!

There are also many country hazards which affect life and limb that give rise to 'complaints'. Most people are aware that bulls can be dangerous - not necessarily if you are wearing red, for they are colour blind! But cows, sheep or goats when protecting their young can turn very nasty, especially to strangers and dogs. Many farmhands have blackened and thickened toenails where cows have trodden on them over the years. And bruises from kicking cows become part of many a dairy farmer's routine expectancy.

Always be wary of walking behind a horse; as my father used to recite:

> The horse it had two legs behind
> And two it has before.
> You walk behind and it's then you find
> What the two behind are for!

Another kind of 'kick' was that given by old tractors. Before the age of batteries and starter motors they had to be cranked into life by hand. A special lever 'retarded' the timing of the ignition spark from the magneto. As soon as the engine was running the timing lever was 'advanced' and all was well. But woe betide anyone who cranked up with the lever 'advanced'. The engine would 'backfire' and wrench the starting handle into reverse, dislocating a novice's thumbs, spraining his wrists or cracking his knee caps! To help prevent this, later starting handles or their sockets were bevelled on the reverse side so that a backfire disengaged the handle.

The prolonged spell of wet weather throughout June this year initiated another irritant that has seriously affected many country people - mosquitoes. They breed freely in the puddles and pools and one strain which seems to have become particularly vicious this summer has already resulted in many swollen arms and legs.

Then there are all those rheumaticky joints, the result of years of working in the rain, those bad backs caused by constant lifting, and hernias that are only kept in check by a good old fashioned wide and low-slung belt.

Yet for all the problems and complaints that arise to distress those of us who live and work in the countryside, fortunately they only seem to arrive one at a time, and over the years perhaps small doses of infection build up an immunity against an outbreak of more serious disease. Perhaps that's why country life is healthier - it's just that those who still have 'complaints' haven't lived long enough to outlive them!

76 August Primitive Privies
GRANNY FACED A FIFTY YARD DASH TO 'SPEND A PENNY'

It can still be found at the bottom of the occasional garden. No, not a family of fairies - but a primitive privy! Although most are usually overgrown with ivy and half-hidden by nettles, some remain functional and a few are even still in daily use.

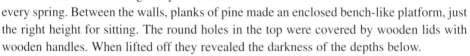

On the farm where I was born, you had to cross the farmyard, go around the far side and back of the black-tarred 'gig' house, then up three steps. It was a journey of at least 50 yards - whether you were in a hurry or not.

The rickety wooden door hung from leather hinges tacked on with large-headed felt nails and was never fastened. Inside was an atmosphere of ecclesiastical cleanliness, for it was religiously whitewashed every spring. Between the walls, planks of pine made an enclosed bench-like platform, just the right height for sitting. The round holes in the top were covered by wooden lids with wooden handles. When lifted off they revealed the darkness of the depths below.

Our privy was a bit unusual. It had the customary seat with a large hole for adults. This was worn smooth by constant use and weekly scrubbing. But beside it and on a lower level was a little hole - for baby bottoms - all rough and uncomfortable around the edges because so few children had used the seat before me.

When I was very young I found it a frightening place and had to be accompanied on my urgent errands by my mother or granny. On arrival they would sit patiently beside me, utilising their enforced idleness and the other seat to advantage whilst waiting for me! As I grew older I also grew bolder and by the time I started school was 'grown up' enough to use even the 'big hole' on my own without the fear of falling through. Through the ever-open door I gazed out onto the glories of the vegetable garden on a summer's day or shivered whilst watching the shooting stars on a frosty night.

The biggest shock I ever had was one night when I paid a visit without the lantern. I sat dreaming about monsters and how courageously I would defend myself if attacked. Then suddenly something damp and furry landed on my lap. I was petrified - until I realised it was only one of our farmyard cats that had silently crept in for a cuddle and a bit of comfort. So much for my courage!

We didn't have toilet rolls in those days - except when we expected visitors. We used sheets of newspaper torn into four, skewered near the corner and strung up with string. They hung from a nail in the wall. When I started to read comics they suffered the same fate. I would sit there for ages engrossed in the task of fitting the pictures back into place again. Alas, only to find that the last and most important part of the story was missing.

There was a wide hole at ground level at the rear of the privy. If its shutter became rusty, rotten or unfastened, the north wind would whistle through with so much force it would even blow the lids off the holes. It also made the daily excursion both draughty and dangerous. Although this hole in the wall was designed to aid the annual emptying of the closet, it also opened up the possibility of my cousins and I playing a prank on anyone we didn't like while they were 'sitting on the throne'. With gloved hands we would tie a bunch of nettles to the end of a long whippy stick, then quietly and carefully poke it inwards and upwards through the hole! The unfortunate victim, who had probably just lapsed into the realms of worldly oblivion, suddenly had his dreams shattered and his senses severely stung. He would leap from the loo like a lion, roaring with rage, and dash out after us, pulling up his trousers as he ran. We lads knew we had to make ourselves scarce for the next hour or two at least - or think up a very convincing alibi.

In towns, special teams of men periodically emptied the earth closets, cesspits, and the buckets which superseded them. Because they performed this task during the hours of darkness the product became known as 'night-soil'. To avoid the nuisance of also having to carry lanterns they worked one week on either side of the full moon. Anybody who asked the team where they were going would received the reply, "We're going to a wedding." Hence the origin of the saying, "I thought I was going to a wedding until I found I was following the muck cart."

It was very inconvenient going to the bottom of the garden in bad weather or at night, so householders purchased specially made ceramic containers (from the Potteries) for use in their bed-chambers. These 'chamber-pots' were emptied, in more recent times, into white enamelled slop buckets fitted with a fluted lid.

In the country the contents were poured onto the compost heap as it is one of nature's best activators. But in the towns the streets once acted as sewers. There the housewives threw out the contents of the chamber-pots from the windows of the overhanging upper storeys with the warning "Gardy Loo", from the French "Gare de l'eau", which roughly translated means "beware" or "look out - water". Anyone who did 'look out' got drenched!

This practice gave rise to the custom that the lady always walked on the inside under cover of the jettied houses, whilst the gentleman walked on the outside - exposed and vulnerable to any sudden deluge. However, fashion provided a partial protection when men took to wearing wide-brimmed hats!

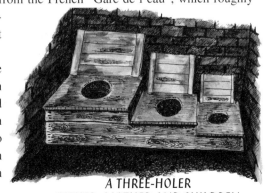

A THREE-HOLER
FATHER, MOTHER AND CHILDREN

With improved hygiene the warning "Gardy Loo" became almost obsolete. What little of the expression remains now signifies the name of the smallest room in the house - the 'loo'. Yet I well remember that on my way to school I passed one ancient roadside cottage where the practice of emptying the slops from the bedroom windows still continued. I always had to be careful which way the wind was blowing before I cycled past, for she gave no warning. But to her credit, in her front garden grew some of the tallest hollyhocks in the district.

With the introduction of a plentiful supply of piped water the sanitary arrangements of the countryside changed. The cold, draughty and inconvenient earth closet or privy was replaced by a flush toilet inside the house. Everything now disappeared into a septic tank sunk out of sight and out of mind until something went wrong with the system!

Yet water has frequently played an important role in the disposal and dispersal of our waste products. Occupants of halls and castles simply tipped theirs into the surrounding moat - which was usually stagnant and frequently stank, though this may have helped to dissuade an enemy from attacking!

Another item of interest is that in Continental countries, where they had early communal toilets, the people were largely illiterate. To separate the sexes the 'Ladies' was denoted by the female symbol of a crescent moon cut through the upper part of the door. A large round hole representing the masculine sun was for 'Gentlemen'. A much simpler system existed on the farms in England; men used the stables and dairymaids the cowshed. And even today some old farmhands will tell you they're just going to water the horses!

But if you are still wondering why our ancestors put the privy at the bottom of the garden - it was so that it would not contaminate the well, which was usually just outside the back door. Ours was at the farm, and I can picture the scene even now, my old granny sipping her cup of hot senna pod tea, already attired in her 'high tops', waiting to do the 50 yards dash' to 'the loo'.

77 September The Ghost of the 'Golden Cross'
UNSOLVED MYSTERY OF 'GHOST' ON THE LANDING

My wife and I recently returned from holiday, having had a very enjoyable week 'away from it all'. Fortunately, my younger son was able to take a break from his engineering work to milk the cows and keep the farm ticking over, whilst his girlfriend was kept busy coping with a constant stream of 'bed and breakfast' guests.

But even on holiday I couldn't escape from the routine of my monthly article and kept wondering what to write about next. It wasn't until we returned that a suitable subject emerged. For however much we had enjoyed our holiday - "there's no place like home." So this month I'll give you an insight into the story of my farmhouse, The Golden Cross.

Ramblers roaming the footpaths of my fields on the Redesmere walk, cyclists pedalling past on the 'Cheshire trail', motorists seeking clues for their charity treasure hunt and visitors to the church who are welcome to wander around our garden nearly always comment on the same subject. "The Golden Cross - that's an unusual name for a farm. It sounds more like a pub."

And they are quite right, for that is what it used to be. The pub and the church are usually found close together at the centre of the village. One catered for the needs of this life, the other for the needs of the next, and I'll leave you to work out which was which!

It was either by a stroke of good luck or a flash of foresight that someone sited this house here. On each side it is sheltered by rising ground, allowing the worst of the wind to whistle over the rooftops. At the top of the garden the church stands four square against the elements. Below the garden the babbling Snape Brook meanders its winding way, first into the Peover Eye then on into the Weaver before merging with the Mersey.

Our house has all the hallmarks of antiquity. The floors are uneven, the ceilings sag, no two adjoining walls are ever square, the damp course is non-existent and the gnarled oak beams are as hard as iron. Yet for all its faults it is a very happy place to live in and it is as full of history as it is of character.

Lying hidden from view underneath the original inn are four cellars, two of them quite large. In them the barrels of beer were kept at a constant temperature. At working height around the walls are large stone slabs. During the winter these were covered with apples for puddings, pumpkins for pies, marrows for stuffing and potatoes for mashing. But the stones also held a much more sobering secret.

Until about 120 years ago the publican was also the village butcher. On those slabs were severed and stored the slices and joints that were waiting to be sold in the shop above. And in one dark corner still remains the old wooden 'turnel' in which pigs were scalded to remove their bristles. Two separate flights of stairs lead up from the cellars to the ground floor and, to save space, immediately above them are the treads and risers of the stairs that run up to the bedrooms.

One entrance to the house is between privet hedges and up seven cement steps to the front door, but in 30 years it has only been used twice. Needless to say, the hinges are stiff with disuse and the bolts are almost seized with layers of paint. Inside the door is now a small hall but originally it was the most important room in the house - the bar. When we first decorated it we were amazed to discover rows of wooden pegs behind the paper on one wall. Then it dawned on us, they were the sawn off remnants of previously protruding pegs. It used to be the rule that each customer had his own tankard which, when not in use, hung from his own peg.

A split 'stable' type door led into a passageway. The top opened inwards and the drink was served over the lower half, which is itself of interest. Along the bottom edge a large semicircular hole suggests that a rat was once eager to get in - or to get out. The front of the door has also been used to test a branding iron and in two instances the initials T.W. are burnt into the wood.

Slightly differing levels on the floors which correspond to similar fluctuations on the ceilings show that a passageway once ran along the centre of the house and divided it up into even smaller 'snug' rooms than we have now. Another passage led into the 'shop' and across to the main staircase. It was entered by a door that has long since been bricked up. The 'shop' had a large wood-burning fireplace. The ceiling beam continued right through the chimney breast. From its hooks were hung bacons and hams to smoke. At some time this beam must have smouldered away, for there are severe scorch marks next to where a newer section is bolted and scarfe jointed onto the original, a couple of feet into the room.

In 1859 the farmer, butcher and landlord William Walker was killed in a riding accident at "Walker's hollow" on the road to Macclesfield. His widow, Ellen, continued as landlady and farmer of the $33^{1}/_{2}$ acres for a further dozen years. When she died the licence was not renewed and the tenancy was taken by Richard Goodwin, the local miller, whose descendants continued until my arrival.

An extension was built onto the roadside end of the inn and what is now our large, glass-fronted, light and airy kitchen was originally an open dairy. The 'living room' had a large black-leaded kitchen range and the exceptional thickness of the wall beside it turned out to be the position of former bake ovens - information which we put to good use a few years ago when we had a central heating unit installed, for the old bakehouse chimney has become the new boiler flue. The present living room used to house the cheese vat and press. The moulded cheeses were put into a lift (still in position) and hoisted upstairs to mature in what is now our bathroom!

Of course no history of any old house would be complete without its resident ghost. We had one series of eerie sounds that took several months to solve. Occasionally by day and frequently by night fairy-like tinkling and distant clangings could be heard, especially in the bathroom. We tapped the pipes, checked the water pressure, looked under the floorboards, all to no avail. The explanation eventually proved to be very simple! We had a canary in a cage. Every time it tinkled its bell the sound travelled from the cage up its suspending chain, through the hook in the ceiling, along the joist into which it was screwed, and vibrated the bath water pipes above, which amplified the sound!

That's the one we discovered - the other remains a mystery. At night, light footsteps creak across the landing and pass along the passageway outside our bedroom door. We've heard it so often that we no longer take any notice and luckily our guests think it is someone going to the bathroom - so it doesn't bother them either!

This old house never seems happier than when it is bustling with activity. In the 1861 census ten people lived here, in addition to accommodating travellers as an inn. Generations of Goodwins kept the place happy with their offspring and in the slightly more recent past our three children and many village boys and girls have had endless hours of fun chasing one another up, down and around the two flights of stairs in 'catch me if you can' games, and playing Hide and Seek in the seventeen rooms and the cellar 'frog-holes'.

Two of our three fledglings have long since flown the nest and have homes of their own - and the other may not be long. For a short while the house has seemed almost empty, sombre, silent and still, slumbering on.

Then three years ago the imposed reduction in our milk quota cut our farm income by 10 per cent. Something had to be done in order to survive. Strangely it was a rent rise that resolved the issue. To pay it, we applied for and received permission to take in guests on a 'bed and breakfast' basis and were granted a licence to use our own Guernsey milk for consumption on the premises. So once again the house echoes to the chatter, chuckles and laughter of 'one nighters', passers-by or longer term travellers and tourists just as it used to do over 100 years ago.

But there is an unexpected twist to the end of this story. Since we returned from holiday we have been so inundated with requests for 'emergency' accommodation that on two occasions this past week my wife and I have had to vacate our own bedroom and take up temporary residence at the far end of the house. This has prompted her into post-holiday action! "Why not turn the adjoining junk room into a dressing room-cum-bathroom en-suite?" she said. Without more ado the items that we had savoured and stored for so many years - in case we ever needed them again - have already been sorted and priced  to sell at forthcoming car-boot sales, so the indications are that sometime in the near future we may well be moving bedrooms, and that will start another chapter in the story.

It is also surprising that in the 'comments' column of our visitors' book so many say not just that they've enjoyed their stay and may well be coming back - as many have - but that it's just like "Home from home". You can't get a much better recommendation than that, can you? Ghost or no ghost at The Golden Cross.

78 October Witches

SMASH THAT EGGSHELL, YOU WICKED WITCH!

Are you disabled, deformed or depressed? Have you any warts, moles, blemishes, birthmarks, bumps or scars on your body? Do you suffer from flat feet, painful corns or bunions? Are you left-handed or cross-eyed? Do you ever lose your temper, swear, chase mischief-making children, fondle a pet or miss church services? Are you ever grumpy, do you mumble under your breath and has anyone a grudge against you?

Because if the answer to any one of these questions is YES and you had lived

between 1200 and 1750AD, YOU might have been accused of being a 'witch'.

If you ate a soft boiled egg the shell always had to be smashed afterwards, for it was claimed that otherwise a witch might use the empty shell to row out to sea. There she would whistle up the wind and cause a storm which might sink a sailing ship and drown the sailors! And why would the sailors drown? Because YOU hadn't smashed your eggshell. For as the poem goes,

> O never leave your eggshells unbroken in the cup
> But think of us poor mariners who always smash them up.
> For witches come and use them, and sail away to sea
> And make a lot of misery for mariners like me!

People believed that witches could wreak havoc with hailstones and ruin growing crops. Farmers blamed witches when animals failed to thrive, when a cow gave blood in its milk, milk turned sour or butter failed to 'come'. A cow that went dry prematurely was said to have been milked into a sieve or a bottomless bucket by a witch. They were also blamed when hens stopped laying, or when hatching eggs failed to produce chicks - a spell that could be broken if all the eggs were marked with an X before incubating, the power of the cross being greater than the power of evil.

The reign of Queen Elizabeth I saw the outbreak of a serious eye complaint which caused cattle to go blind. It resulted in the condemnation and death of many bewitching 'eye-biters'. We now believe it was 'New Forest' disease and spread by flies.

Any problems that couldn't be easily explained were put down to interference by a witch casting a spell. Superstitions against their ill effect were (and still are) widely practised. But the best way to counteract a spell was to stop it at source - kill the witch! The mainstay of the religious persecution was that those who did not conform with the established religion must therefore believe in the teachings of the Devil. And the book of Exodus states, "Thou shalt not suffer a witch to live."

Anyone could be accused - royalty, nobility, priests and judges included. But since men controlled the Church, the government, and the judiciary, the majority of people accused of witchcraft were women. They also had fewer legal rights, were more emotional and were considered less capable of defending themselves against the advances of the Devil. The only 'evidence' required against a person was that their name was written anonymously onto a piece of paper and posted into the thrice-locked witching-chest in the church. The authorities had to interrogate the person so named. The 'accused' had no rights and was considered guilty until he or she proved their own innocence - the exact opposite of our present legal system. If the eventual outcome was "Guilty", as it almost invariably was, whoever had spoken in favour of them automatically became suspect and were similarly examined. For this reason it was rare to have a defending lawyer or indeed anyone to speak out in their favour.

Abused, confused, often not even knowing the charge against them, they were stripped in public, shaved of all hair, then questioned by expert interrogators, who also examined them minutely for the tell-tale 'devil's-mark'. These were any wart, mole mark or scar from which a pet or 'familiar' might suck life-giving blood. Long pins or prickers were prodded into suspected areas; if the accused failed to scream that was a likely site of the 'devil's mark' and they were therefore pronounced guilty.

Some judges even resorted to trickery by using a special pricker with a blade which retracted into the handle to obtain false results and faster confessions. Others promised leniency if the accused confessed. But the promise was never kept, for no-one need keep a promise made to a witch. When the verdict was "Guilty" the 'witch' was taken out and hanged, unless the accusation was "heresy" - against the church, or "treason" - against the state, when the 'witch' was tied to a stake, stacked around with brushwood and burned alive, as was Joan of Arc.

Trials were also conducted by fire and water. In the trial by fire the accused had to stand on the north (Devil's) side of the church altar throughout the service of Mass or, later, Holy Communion. When all except the accused had partaken of the sacrament, he or she had to grab hold of a red hot iron bar which had been heated over a brazier and walk three paces southwards across the face of the altar (Father, Son and Holy Ghost). The bar was dropped and the blistered hands bandaged. Seven days later at the end of the service the hands were unbandaged. If the wounds had festered, the verdict was "Guilty". If clean and healing, "Innocent" and the sacrament was then given to them.

Another equally painful version to prove innocence was to retrieve a silver coin from the bottom of a bucket of boiling water. If you failed after three attempts you were guilty. A less painful alternative, introduced later, was to be weighed against the Church Bible. Providing the Bible proved heavier, you were innocent. So lightweights survived and heavyweights perished!

The trial by water, known as 'swimming a witch', was also supervised by the clergy. With arms crossed and thumbs tied to big toes (and sometimes bundled into a bag), the accused was thrown into deep water. The theological theory was that the water would reject anything evil and cause it to float. So if the accused floated they were guilty and were put to death. If they sank they were innocent - but had usually drowned by the time the authorities allowed them to be dragged out!

Torture had been approved by the Vatican since 1257. Most towns and large villages had a ducking stool. The unfortunate wretch was strapped in and repeatedly lowered into the cold water, often in the depths of winter, until a suitable confession was obtained.

Forced feeding with extremely salted beef and allowing no water was another method. Sadistic devices imposed extreme physical torment, while mental pain was exerted by keeping the 'witch' awake until a garbled confession emerged.

Many died under the rigours of these tortures. Most people quickly made false confessions. This large number of false confessions gave the judiciary the impression that witchcraft was far more widespread than it actually was and they attacked the supposed problem with renewed vigour, often with substantial financial reward. For if and when found guilty, 'witches' had all their possessions confiscated. The cost of imprisonment, torture, trial and hanging or burning was deducted and the judge pocketed the rest for himself. If the 'witch' left no belongings, his or her relatives had to fork out instead or they would become suspect.The judge was also rewarded with a payment of twenty shillings (£1) for every 'witch' found guilty - and that was called Justice.

Who were the witches? Despite the numerous stories which emerged during the witch hunts, very few people of sound mind were ever proved to have "sold their soul to Satan". But many did still follow their former Celtic ('witch') gods of Odin and Wodan.

One of the familiar forms that the witch was believed to transform herself into. Could this be why the bat is still feared by many people today.

Others rebelled against authority of any kind and did not join in with the traditions and customs of their fellow citizens. Then there were those who dabbled in the occult for profit or the sheer 'devilment' of it. Add to them the mentally sick who imagined they were possessed by demons or lived a twilight life that couldn't differentiate between dreams and reality, the elderly, infirm, ugly and cranky who were no longer 'required' by society - in fact anyone who was not in every way normal might be feared and condemned as a 'witch'.

Very few were actually 'guilty'. Aren't you glad we now live in an enlightened age?

79 November For Whom the Bell Tolls
OLD CUSTOMS THAT GAVE DEATH A HELPING HAND

Throughout history the success of our evolution has been based upon "the survival of the fittest". Although this extremely wet season has devastated us, if our ancestors had suffered a similar fate their food stocks would soon have been hovering around starvation level. To compensate for the calamity, to economise on the consumption of corn and thereby to try to reduce the risk of an almost certain disaster, **all** animals that were not essential for the future working and stocking of the countryside would have been slaughtered around St Martinmas - November 11th. This would have allowed the scant supplies to be shared out between the survivors.

But are you aware that until this last century it also applied to **people** who had outlived their usefulness? As November is traditionally regarded as the month of the dead I thought that this might be the appropriate time to tell you about it and some of the other curious customs connected with those who were "dispatched." The term that was most frequently used on such occasions was "easing the passing". It took several forms.

Country cottages were usually one-room hovels with a beaten earth floor. If the ailing person was having difficulty dying, the commonest practice was simply to lift them out of their warm bed and lay them on the cold floor. And sure enough, within a few hours the end would come - "easier". People had no knowledge of hypothermia; they believed that as we all originated out of the earth, so the earth would welcome our return. As the Book of Common Prayer puts it, "Earth to earth, ashes to ashes and dust to dust."

If a person was less willing to "let go", another way of achieving the same end was to tie a broad band around the neck and put a stick in the knot. Every few minutes the stick was turned; over a short period, the person would lose consciousness and finally be asphyxiated!

However, there were a series of superstitions which had to be strictly adhered to, to help the soul of the departed to escape, or their spirit might return to haunt them. One of these fallacies was that at the moment of 'passing', the soul would leave the body and try to wing its way upward towards Paradise and so be saved. Unfortunately, there were Evil Spirits lurking everywhere who might capture the soul in flight and drag it down into the torment of the underworld, or Hell as it was later called. There was a way round this problem. It was thought that Evil Spirits could not stand the sound of bells, which is why they were always rung before church services - originally to scare unwanted spirits out of

earshot and thus make the area more holy!

This belief was put into practice by the relatives. The churchwarden was warned to stand by to ring the 'passing bell' in about an hour as 'so and so' was on their way out. The bell was rung three times for a child, six times for a woman and nine times for a man ("Nine 'tailors' (tellers) for a man").

Why the variants, you may ask? Children had three bells for the Trinity - to warn the Father, Son and Holy Ghost that they were on their way. Ladies required six strokes and then single strokes denoting their age - because the older they were the heavier would be their weight of sins and the longer it would take them to reach safety. Men had most sins to bear and, being the heaviest burdened, would take the longest time to get there; therefore the bells had to be run over a longer period!

But there arose another problem! If the churchwarden was disturbed from his slumbers and had to ring the bell at night he charged seven pence, but during daylight hours it only cost four pence! So whoever was "ebbing away", the family tried to make sure that they lingered on at least until daybreak, for it would save them three pence - which was as good as the 'divi' in olden days.

Yet another problem emerged. Suppose the warden had been warned to ring the bell in an hour - he did - and at the end of the ringing the ailing person was still alive. The money had been wasted and the evil spirits would surely snatch the soul when it did "pass". So the next problem to solve was how to make sure that the person died at the precise moment that the bells were being rung.

To achieve this aim ancient churches had a hook on the wall behind the door. From that hook hung the 'Holy Mawle' - a large wooden mallet! When the churchwarden was informed the 'Holy Mawle' was taken home. The family would listen out for the 'passing bell'. At the first stroke the dying person would receive several heavy blows on the head from the mallet, ensuring that they 'passed' at the moment that the 'passing bell' was being rung. Everyone wished to get to heaven so no one complained if the family helped them on their way. And no doctor of old would ever have dared to challenge such disposals as anything but 'normal' under the circumstances.

The other main method was known as the 'passing pillow'. Most parishes owned one. They were deep, they were edged with black lace and they were filled with dove feathers. Why? Well, when Jesus was being baptised in the River Jordan, the Holy Spirit descended onto his shoulder in the form of a dove. A dove has feathers, so dove feathers symbolised the Holy Spirit! And the superstition was (until very recently) that you can't die on feathers - the religious reason for placing the "passing" person on the floor!

In this case, when the churchwarden was informed, the 'passing pillow' was taken home and the head of the dying person was placed upon it. A listen was kept and at the first stroke of the bell the 'passing pillow' was snatched away - jerking the head of the dying so drastically that death generally followed immediately. If the sudden shock did not bring about the end, then the pillow was placed over the face until "passing" was completed. This ceremony is also listed as "drawing the pillow" - WITHdrawing the pillow!

By ancient custom there was also a way that the dead person's load of sin could be lightened to allow a more rapid ascent. A plate of food containing plenty of butter was placed on the chest of the corpse. It was thought that the sins of the deceased would be absorbed by the food. For a small payment, a few hours later the poor, but professional, village "sin-eater" would consume the food in the presence of the corpse, thereby transferring the sins of the dead upon themselves - in a similar way to the ritual formerly accomplished by the 'scapegoat'.

Wine was also given. Each drop represented one sin and many a lifeless corpse might well have been shocked had they seen the supposed magnitude of their sins!!!

In case you think these stories are a bit far-fetched, may I point out that 'Holy Mawles' still occasionally come to light. These mallets often bear an inscription: "This person died that the children might not be deprived of their bread."

The last recorded use of the 'passing pillow' took place in a village in the Isle of Ely in 1902. That pillow was supposed to have been made by a nun.

Although the custom of 'sin-eating' diminished in Victorian times, I have actually met people who have witnessed the ceremony!

So if at any time life is looking gloomy, you are feeling poorly and are confined to bed, if anyone should ask you, "Would you like another pillow to prop you up?" - don't you let them; they might snatch it away!

Or if you suffer from "water on the brain" mind they don't get the chance to give you "a TAP on the head", especially if you happen to hear ringing noises in your ears!!!

80 December The Origins of Christmas
HOW SANTA'S GOLD SAVED THREE PRETTY GIRLS

In Rome our early Christian ancestors celebrated the "Birth of Christ" on many different dates during the formulative years of our religion. The 1st and 6th of January, the 25th of March and the 29th of September were all tried for short periods. But largely due to religious persecution they never became established.

About 342AD they tried again. This time they chose the 25th day of the tenth month (December), the Roman festival of "the birth of the unconquered sun" and the Phrygian sun god Mithras. They succeeded - largely because it also came at the end of the seven day Roman feast of Saturnalia (the god of peace and plenty). After a week of orgies and bouts of heavy eating and drinking, the citizens were suffering from such a hangover that they were in no fit condition to pursue and arrest a few Christian dissidents! So the feast of the 'Sun God' became the festival of the 'Son of God'.

As the new religion spread northwards the great mid-winter celebration of Yule was also gradually superseded by Christmas. By 440AD the holy day was so firmly established that the Christian Church made 25th December official and ordered everyone to condition themselves for this annual festival by a period of forty days of preparation (similar to Lent) to herald the birthday of the baby Jesus. This season they called "Advent", which means "the coming". Nowadays Advent starts on the Sunday nearest to November 30th (St Andrew's Day) and, although much shorter, it is still regarded by the church as an important period.

Sadly, today many people forget this religious side of the festivities. They leave "Christ" out of "Christmas" - then complain that the festival doesn't mean anything to them anymore! Yet there is no reason why they should not enjoy both aspects of the festive season.

How has all this 'modern' razzmatazz come about? In fact, some of it has always been there. Throughout history, 'Christmas' has absorbed so many beliefs and fables, customs and characters that the festival has now grown into a hotch-potch of almost inextricably interlaced religion and commerce.

During the seven days of the Roman feast of Saturnalia (19th to 25th December) houses were decorated with greenery, and lamps were repositioned to give special lighting effects. Masters and servants swapped roles - a custom still commemorated in the forces today when the officers serve the men with their Christmas dinner. On 25th December - *Dies natalis invicti solis* ("the birth of the unconquered sun") - the Romans paraded through the streets carrying a statue of a virgin holding her child! This was followed by the Feast of the Juvenalia, which in medieval Britain became the Feast of the Innocents.

Roman consuls were elected during the first days of January which were called The Feast of the Kalends (from which we get our word 'calendar'). Everywhere was again lit and decorated and special presents called Strenia (after the goddess of strength) were exchanged between adults and other presents were given to children. The events of the past year were mulled over and divinations predicted of what the new year held in store. Men danced in the streets wearing animal skins and disguised with blackened faces, customs perpetuated by the 'Guisers' and Mummers' plays and by the Horn dances that still linger in our rural areas.

At the end of December the Jews held a Hanukkah - a 'festival of lights'. One candle was lit on the first day, two on the second, until all eight burned on the eighth day - to remember the building of Solomon's temple. Games were played and presents exchanged. The early Christians suggested that the shepherds brought gifts to Jesus on the first Christmas morn, as did the three wise men who later came from the East - on their camels!

In Northern Europe the icy mid-winter solstice was celebrated by the fire festival of Yule. The Celts thought that the sun had gone to sleep, so to keep Jack Frost at bay they hauled great yule logs onto their fires and held noisy gatherings to try to revive the sun. They believed that the black-bearded Odin (or Woden) rumbled around the heavens in his chariot of molten gold drawn by his horses, Allstrong and Early Waker. When earthbound he rode his famous, huge, white, eight-legged horse, Sleipir. On windy, wintry nights he howled around the houses in the Herlathing - hunting for any naughty children, whom he carried away. To appease him, people put out grain, to feed Sleipir, and food for Woden and his accompanying spirits from Valhalla (now food to feed the reindeer and a sherry and mince pie for Santa!). During the mid-winter solstice a boar was sacrificed and its head ceremonially eaten in honour of Woden's wife Freya (Friday), the goddess of fertility. In the boar's mouth was a round, red apple, later replaced by an orange - to represent the sun (shades of Mithras?).

Many of these ancient customs linger on, welded together in the newer festival of Christmas. Apart from the baby Jesus, probably the best-known character is Santa Claus. His story starts some 1700 years ago at Patara in Turkey. When Nicholas was young, his parents perished in an epidemic. He took to the priesthood, gave away his inherited fortune and became Bishop of Myra, a district visited by St Paul some 200 years previously.

The legend about St Nicholas that concerns us is of the nobleman who fell on such hard times that he could no longer offer a dowry for his three beautiful daughters. Instead, he would have to sell them into slavery. The saintly priest heard of his plight and on three successive nights secretly threw a bag of gold in through the windows. The daughters, now with suitable dowries, married satisfactorily and lived happily ever after.

There our story would end, had it not been for the fact that one of the bags of gold landed in the young lady's slipper which was warming by the fire. Which is why, ever after, European children were encouraged to put their slippers, shoes or clogs by the fireside on St Nicholas's Day, December 6th. The Dutch, in particular, took this custom to America. They founded New Amsterdam, which is now New York, and continued giving their children presents on Saint Claus's day. However, clogs became replaced by lace-up boots, which were difficult to fill, so stockings were hung up instead!

English colonials and troops returning from America tried to introduce the custom into England but without success. During the Industrial Revolution, when workers were paid on piecework, they could only afford one day off at Christmas. It was no longer the happy 'Feast of Fools' fortnight of romp and frolic of former times. Children worked twelve hours a day or longer, in the dark Satanic mills or cleaning chimneys.

Only after Queen Victoria came to the throne was there any change of heart. By then people were becoming more prosperous, there was a resurgence of religion and reforming zeal, and children became the objects of sympathy and concern. Until then, only the wealthy had exchanged presents at Christmas; now at last children received them too - not on St Nicholas's Day but on 25th December instead - but still brought by the 'Americanized' figure of Santa Claus and put into their stocking, which for some changed into a pillow case. Industrialists, shopkeepers and craftsmen saw an opportunity for expansion and with the added attraction of the stories by Charles Dickens the commercialisation of Christmas had begun.

However, hovering in the background was yet another character waiting to team up with the festivities. The medieval mummers had a narrator who also doubled as a doctor. He was holly-crowned, red-faced, ribald and rakish; his name - "Father Christmas"! Somewhere along the line he and Santa Claus became intertwined. His image was smartened, with a white beard, red tunic and cap, in the 1860s, by the American artist Thomas Nast illustrating the story of 1809 by Washington Irving which itself led to Clement Moore's famous poem of 1823:

> 'Twas the night before Christmas when all through the house,
> Not a creature was stirring, not even a mouse.
> The stockings were hung by the chimney with care,
> In hopes that St. Nicholas soon would be there.

Later the poem mentions a sleigh which flew through the air - pulled by eight reindeer: Dasher and Dancer, Prancer and Vixen, Comet and Cupid, Donner and Blitzen. Rudolph is a more recent addition.

"Down the chimney St Nicholas came with a bound" - then he filled all the stockings with toys from a pack on his back!

So, just in case he calls, don't forget to hang your stocking up - or at least leave your slippers to warm in front of the fire. And may you find them filled with what you most desire - warm feet? A very happy festive season to you and yours but please DON'T LEAVE CHRIST out of CHRISTMAS.

81 January 1988 ...And so to Bed
AND SO TO BED.... WITH A TASSEL TO FOOL THE WITCHES

It is a little-appreciated fact that people who reach their mid-70s have spent about 25 years in BED! And incidentally, as far as I am aware, man is the only species of the animal kingdom that lies on its back when asleep and gives its position away - by snoring - as my wife constantly reminds me.

There is a well-known rhyme: "Early to bed, Early to rise, Makes a man healthy, wealthy and wise".

Early to bed was certainly the rule in olden times. The curfew (French: *couvre-feu* - cover fire) rang at 8pm every night in the winter and 9pm every night of the summer. This meant that by law all fires had to be covered overnight to prevent sparks spitting out and setting the straw or rush floor covering alight. Because the fire was the centre of light and warmth in the household, once it was covered most folk went to bed. Country people worked from dawn to dusk, which although in itself was not physically hard, when coupled with the tiring effect of wind and weather, they were probably glad to "hit the hay" at night.

Yet not all was peace and tranquillity, as 14th century "Piers Plowman" reminds us:
"The peasant spent the dark hours of a stormy wet night searching around
his poorly thatched hovel trying to find a dry spot to rest his tired body,
whilst having to rock the cradle to quell the cries of his wakeful offspring."

He probably slept on a 'truckle' - a straw mattress. Until this century these were regularly made on site by shepherds at lambing time and itinerant labourers who journeyed

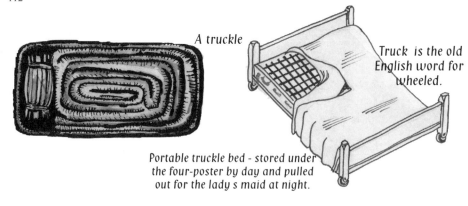

A truckle

Truck is the old English word for wheeled.

Portable truckle bed - stored under the four-poster by day and pulled out for the lady s maid at night.

around farms seeking seasonal work. The farmer would provide a couple of trusses of straw which the workers wound into a long, soft straw-rope using a 'wimble', 'scud winder' or 'throw-hook'. The rope was coiled tightly around itself, making an oblong mat slightly longer than the man's height and wider than his width. It was held flat by skewering it through with spiked willow spics. The coils were then stitched together with a curved stack needle and split bramble lengths. A couple of rounds were sewn above the outside layer; they formed a lip to keep the blankets in and the draughts out. A log of wood or a bag of chaff provided the pillow, and hemp sacking the blankets.

Hall stewards, inn-keepers and farmers would often keep one or two ready-made for children, unexpected guests or expectant mothers! When mounted on a castored carriage they were called 'trundles' because they 'trundled' under the bed for storage. Maids slept on them if their mistress was nervous of being alone at night.

In the ancient halls the nobility had ground level bedchambers which adjoined the main hall. Their wide entrances were screened with leather curtains for privacy. Servants slept on the straw and rushes around the central fire.

When 'half-lofts' were built in taller houses and halls the older and more agile children climbed up the vertical 'granny-ladder' affixed to the wall to the bedroom above. The big breakthrough came when instead of going 'up a ladder' to the second storey people went 'upstairs'. Then bedrooms really came into fashion.

To keep the bed above the draughts they were raised on four feet, but there was a much more serious problem. Ceilings had not yet been invented and at night rats and mice would scurry along the rafters under the thatch. They weren't particular what they did or where they did it! The remedy was to erect four posts at the corners of the bed to hold an overhead canopy to catch the droppings! And that was the original purpose of having a 'four-poster' bed. A secondary use soon emerged when curtains were hung between the posts. Most people imagine this was primarily to keep out the draughts. Not so! Bedrooms were interconnecting. To reach the last room people passed through the previous ones, so the original reason for curtains was privacy!

However, the bed was now an enclosed area within the bedchamber and as a result did become warmer. It also kept out the cold night air, which was once thought to be very dangerous to health!

On visiting stately houses today you may have noticed that the 'four-poster' bed curtains are tied back with cords which have a 'tassel' at the end. They were purposely put there to stop witches casting spells on the occupants while they slept! The idea was that should a witch enter she would so enjoy playing with your 'tassel' that she would forget to put a spell on you!

Four-poster beds needed a base (I nearly said a bottom). This was provided by a criss-cross of ropes. In time the ropes became slack, the bed sagged and the occupants rolled into the middle! The problem was rectified by stretching the ropes taut and re-knotting the ends, after which you could once again, as the saying suggests, "sleep tight"!

On top of the ropes lay the woven matting of rushes or straw on which people slept. But for greater comfort short goose feathers were collected, sterilised and stuffed into a large linen (flax) case to make a 'feather-bed' - the symbol of ease and luxury. In use, these soon became lumpy and had to be turned over and shaken regularly, though not on a Friday or Saturday, for bad dreams would result, nor on a Sunday, for that would bring about bad luck as well as nightmares! The best time was when the moon was on the wane. Its powers of attraction were then least and the feathers would lay down more evenly.

Special wooden 'smoothers' of *Lignum vitae* were used to level the bed daily. They were often given as bridal presents. After use, they were placed on each side of the bed to stop the bedclothes slipping off. Another purpose to which they were put was to practise swordfighting - instead of a rapier. The saying, "In the twinkling of an eye" was formerly, "In the twinkling of a bedpost", and before that, "In the twinkling of a bed staff" (as fast as the flicker of a rapier).

Beds had coverlets and counterpanes upon them. Winchester became famous for some of the early woollen ones. Young maidens would spin and weave their own napery - table and bed linen - before marriage, whilst still a 'spinster'.

By Tudor times the woodwork of the four-poster was intricately carved and the counterpanes, bedspreads, curtains, top and bottom valences (short curtains) became beautifully embroidered. Indeed, one Royal bed of silver thread on crimson velvet cost £8,000 and that was before the days of inflation.

The higher up the world you were in status, the higher up in bed, too. Rich people had two or three mattresses beneath them. To 'climb' into bed they needed steps - which doubled as a night commode. Travelling noblemen even had their own portable beds which could be drawn by horses.

On occasions in our history the rich and royalty sometimes stayed in bed all day, receiving courtiers and conducting business from them and not rising until after 5pm.

Because mourning was taken so seriously and lasted so long, even beds, canopies and curtains were draped with black for months on end. Some families possessed a special 'mourning bed' which they rented out to friends and acquaintances when a death occurred.

Beds were frequently the most valuable item of furniture in the household and were often mentioned in wills. However, the poorer the person, the plainer the bed. The lower classes slept on mattresses stuffed with straw or hay. Some used special grasses, ladies' bedstraw and fleabane, mixed with sweet-smelling woodruff and agrimony, wormwood and rose petals, all of which could be replaced cheaply.

Large families with no room to spare led to overcrowding. For extra warmth in winter, children slept several to a bed. They lay alternately head to toe, boys and girls together. There was no segregation of the sexes until adolescence, when separation sometimes occurred - sometimes not!

Special nightclothes were unknown until the 1600s. Before that, people mainly slept naked in summer, and in their workaday clothes in winter. Then to keep the sheets cleaner nightgowns were introduced for ladies and nightshirts for men. Also very important in unheated bedrooms, nightcaps - not the bedtime drink, but a woollen covering that helped to reduce the one-third of body heat that could be lost through the head.

Fireplaces heated the bedrooms of the more affluent. Even so, serving maids were sent to warm the bed before the master retired - by lying in it! Later, brass warming pans which contained hot embers were gracefully guided between the sheets to take off the chill. The next stage was large round stones or firebricks, pre-heated on the hob. They were enclosed in a knitted cover to prevent them burning the skin and were kept in bed overnight. Next came hot water bottles of stone, brass, aluminium and rubber.

Now nearly all these have been superseded by the electric blanket. And between you, me and the bedpost, thank goodness!

Well, it's getting late - the curfew has rung. It's past eight o'clock. I must climb up those wooden hills. For as I said at the beginning - "Early to bed, Early to rise - keeps the red from the whites of your eyes."

82 February Courting Customs
WHEN IT REALLY WAS BED AND BOARD FOR A ROMANTIC ROMEO

February 14th has always been a very important date in the country calendar. Farmers regard it as being almost exactly halfway through the winter. They know that before their animals can be turned out onto grass full time, they will eat the same amount of fodder as they have already consumed.

So to survive through until the Spring the hay barns and silage clamps should still be at least half full.

By tradition February 14th also denotes the day when birds are supposed to choose their mates and start to search for a suitable nesting site. But there is a much more important reason why this date is so widely recognised today. Other birds' - the non-flying variety - receive anonymous messages such as "Roses are red, Violets are blue, Honey is sweet - and so are you." Or "Will you be my Valentine?" As an 'innocent' lad it always puzzled me - how could the recipient return the compliment when there was no name supplied?

In East Anglia I grew up with the custom that any eligible, unattached young maiden might receive a knock on her door after dark. On opening it she found that an admirer had left a package on the doorstep. However there was sometimes an unexpected twist to his generosity. For, as she bent down to pick up the parcel, it was whisked away with a length of line towards the hopeful romantic Romeo who was hiding behind the hedge. Woe betide him, if, instead of his heart's desire, it was the irate father who appeared at the door. That was the signal that his love was lost and he had better show a clean pair of heels very quickly - as I once nearly discovered to my cost.

But how did these curious courting customs come to be celebrated at this time of the year? On February 15th the ancient Romans had a fertility festival called "Lupercalia". It was held in honour of the Lycean God, Pan, who protected the flocks of sheep from the wolves. The ceremonials took place on the site where Romulus, who founded Rome in 753BC, and his twin brother Remus, were reared by their foster mother, a wolf. Sacrifices of goats and dogs were offered to the Gods and then eaten. "And what are little boys made of? Slugs and snails and PUPPY DOG TAILS"1

Afterwards young men of high rank ran amok with thongs of goatskin, whipping and thereby purging all the young women they met to make them fruitful. At the same time further rituals were performed including the selected choice of partners by lot.

It just happened that about a thousand years later St Valentine was honoured on the Eve of Lupercalia. Consequently some of those courting customs clung to the date of his martyrdom, whilst other aspects of the revelry transformed to the Christian festivals of Candlemas and Shrove Tuesday.

Sometimes it was a very serious affair between two individuals, often too shy to pop the question in any other way or on any other day. But in contrast, for many it was simply an additional excuse for a bit of extra fun and frolic, as shown by records which state: "Equal numbers of unattached young men and ladies had their names written on billets of paper which were put separately into a vessel, vase or hat.

Everyone then drew the name of their 'Valentine', which, if the matter was pursued, was thought to be a good omen for a marriage in the future."

Although primarily thought of as a festival where younger people paired up, there were times when it was quite common for consenting married men and women to have and be had as 'Valentines', either by direct choice or by lottery. During the 1660s, the diarist Samuel Pepys refers to this custom several times. On one occasion he wrote that he was quite indignant when he discovered that his wife had drawn him as her 'Valentine' in 'he lottery. As a result he had to buy her a suitable present which cost him five guineas. However he consoled himself by commenting it would have cost him that much whoever his 'Valentine' had been!

The generally expected presents of the day were silk stockings, embroidered garters or gloves; though occasionally expensive jewellery gained more than just a passing affection.

Many a country courtship started at the churchyard kissing gate *and ended up at the altar*

From early times girls were led to believe that they would marry the first bachelor they saw on February 14th and carefully avoided unacceptable candidates. Here again we are told that on St Valentine's Day 1662, Mrs Samuel Pepys covered her eyes all morning to prevent her seeing the painters who were gilding the fireplace, thus possibly having to become their 'Valentine'.

Apart from finding a partner on St Valentine's Day it was the usual practice that the young man would ask for the "hand" of the young lady from her father. But this rule could be broken every fourth year, leap year - when the girl could ask the boy to marry her. If he turned down her request he had to give a suitable present as compensation.

A Scottish ruling of 1288 stated he had to give "One pound - or less, according to his estate, unless he could prove he was already betrothed." The customary gift for rejection in England was a silk gown. If the young man was "caught" all bade well for, "Happy they'll be that wed and wive within leap year, they're sure to thrive."

But coming back to Valentine; should the relationship prove a success the young countryman would plait a special straw shape, often in the form of a lovers' knot. This was called a "hand-fast" or "holdfast" favour. If his lady-love accepted the favour it meant that she accepted him as her fiance and would live with him for a year and a day, the period of the "handfast". If she became pregnant during that time they automatically got married. But if at the end of the year and a day nothing had come of it, the couple separated, each found a fresh partner and tried again, and sometimes again and again. Not much different from today!

Working couples in particular proved themselves fertile first before finally "tying the knot". So common was this practice that babies were not classed as illegitimate provided they were born one month or more after the marriage.

Around the 1700s the church began to object to the "handfast". Not that the authorities were against the couple proving themselves fertile, but rather that, having started a baby on the way, the morals of the young man might start to slip away from the responsibilities of parenthood. Homes were hard to come by. Landlords were demolishing them, either because they couldn't afford repairs, or they wished to enlarge their parklands and provide an unobstructed view, or they were extending their enclosures. Alehouses had increased in number and one of the main topics of conversation in them was that young men could get higher wages in the new mills and factories beginning to be built in the towns. And off they went, leaving the young and unmarried mother high and dry - holding the baby - now classed as illegitimate. This is where the problem arose.

Parliament in its wisdom had decreed that all illegitimate children should, at baptism, become wards of the church and be provided with 'one shilling and half a loaf of bread a week until the child be seven years old and able to fend for itself" - at SEVEN years old!

This money had to come from the church coffers and was a serious drain on the church resources, so a rule was enforced. While the youngsters were 'handfasting", the man was not allowed to remove his breeches in bed, only his boots, and she was not allowed to remove her petticoats! Knickers were not worn until Victorian times. They were originally known as bloomers and were worn in two halves, which is why they are still called 'a pair'. Never heard of half a knicker?

But this did not prove any more effective either and the church was still left holding the baby - for the next seven years. Another attempt was made to restrict the youngsters during the 'handfast". Not only must he retain his breeches, and she her petticoats, but down the centre of the bed was to be placed an upright board - it was once, quite literally, "bed and board"!

But that didn't work either. Still she became pregnant, he left to work elsewhere, and the church was left to maintain the child. Around 1800, the Church's contribution was raised to two shillings a week and since about one child in every seven was now born illegitimate the funds were disastrously low. Yet another custom was introduced. Every night during the duration of the 'handfast" the lower half of the young lady was enclosed in a special loose fitting "bundling" bag - rather like a large sack; in Wales it was called a "stocking'. It was the duty of the girl's mother - or the farmer's wife - to tie the pyjama-like cord of the 'bundling' bag around the girls waist in a series of tight knots. The intention was to protect the young ladies' virtue - but it seldom did!

A few years later Parliament changed the law. But the extinct custom has been handed down to us in the saying that parents still use at bedtime when they tell their children "Come on now, behave yourselves, or I will 'bundle' you off to bed." And in case you think 'bundling' was an archaic custom, it continued in many of the isolated areas of the British Isles until the late 1940s.

Some of the other customs have also changed considerably. The former expensive presents of 'Valentine' have now been replaced by commercially produced cards and the 'handfast' favour of straw has been superceded by the engagement ring of gold. Yet at this time of year a young man's fancy still turns to what his girlfriend has been dreaming about all winter - especially in this, a LEAP YEAR.

So my advice to any young lady who is wondering whether to ask her boyfriend if he will tie the nuptial knot is - "Look before you leap, but if you intend leaping don't look too long - or you may leave it too late."

83 March Children's Games
PAST RITUALS LIVE ON IN CHILDREN'S GAMES

ALTHOUGH, to a lesser extent they still continue today, there was a time, not so very long ago, when every changing season could be identified by the games that children were playing. Like links in an unbroken chain that stretched back through the centuries, children's games have preserved in play the harsh realities of largely forgotten folk beliefs and ancient rituals of work and worship that existed before most written records began.

In a precise order, which to an outsider might defy explanation, at almost the same time every year each game miraculously appeared, and a few days or weeks later, just as mysteriously disappeared - as the next one emerged.

Games were a disciplined way of learning. Each had its own complicated set of rules and regulations which had to be obeyed by all for play to continue. The playground was and still is, the training ground for adulthood, teaching coordination of body and mind, competitiveness and team spirit.

Because games were an innocent re-enactment of life as it was, we can often fathom out some of the deeper half-hidden meanings that they convey. Long forgotten church customs of Lent were recalled by whips and tops. Until the 18th century they were kept in some churches so that sinners could symbolically expel the devil, hardship and their own sins from themselves and their community.

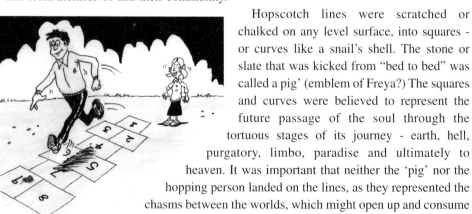

Hopscotch lines were scratched or chalked on any level surface, into squares - or curves like a snail's shell. The stone or slate that was kicked from "bed to bed" was called a pig' (emblem of Freya?) The squares and curves were believed to represent the future passage of the soul through the tortuous stages of its journey - earth, hell, purgatory, limbo, paradise and ultimately to heaven. It was important that neither the 'pig' nor the hopping person landed on the lines, as they represented the chasms between the worlds, which might open up and consume the victim.

And that is why even today some people avoid stepping on the joins in the pavement! The small ups and downs of life were enjoyed sitting astride a plank, pivoted on a larger log or tree trunk. This "see-saw" was often found near a saw-pit, where the materials for making it were readily available. The children mimicked the action of the sawyers.

The frog's method of jumping. with legs wide apart, gave the name to the Spring game of 'leap frogging' over one another's backs. Spring in the air gave a lightness to the feet which made young people want to vault and leap, skip and dance. These, too, were relics of rituals performed to enhance the growth of crops. Children used them as a means to learn their condiments, occupations, materials and alphabet.

Pepper, salt, mustard, vinegar
Tinker, tailor, soldier. sailor
Silk, satin, muslin, rags
A, B, C, D, ...and so on.

Skipping either on their own or with a long swinging rope they would dance in and out, forwards and backwards, singly or in teams. Anyone a bit slow in taking their turn was encouraged to get a move on by the shout "Keep the kettle boiling".

The arrival of May marked the games of fertility associated with the May Queen and the maypole, such as "In and out the windows - as you have done before" and "Here we go gathering nuts in May". The nuts in question were in fact knots or posies of flowers used to decorate and garland the maypole, people's doors and homes. At the conclusion of the song a 'Tug of War took place.

Children copied their elders by playing at kissing and courting, mating and marriage. Seated in a 'symbolically religious' circle one would drop a handkerchief, glove or purse behind a sweetheart's back then try to race round and sit in their place before being 'caught'.

To tell the time children would blow at the rounded 'clock' heads of the dandelion, then gaze in rapture as the tiny seedheads drifted slowly away suspended beneath their downy parachutes.

Buttercups were picked and placed under one another's chin with the question "Do you like butter?" If the answer was a smile and a yellow reflection - they did!

Daisy stalks were split and others pushed through to make "daisy chains" (days-eye).

These they hung around their necks, an honour once reserved only for the Gods or people shortly to be sacrificed to them. At sacred wells, rivers, fountains and dewponds, votive offerings of rags, pins and money were given as an annual tribute to the water spirits. It has now become the Christian custom of 'Well dressing'. But children recall even earlier events in "My Lady's Daughter". Water was taken from the sacred source and flowers were given as payment in the rhyme; but in the actions the last child that went through the arched arms was captured for sacrifice.

Wells were blessed and 'dressed' to prevent them going dry, rivers to counteract disaster from flooding, as occurs in the widely known "London Bridge is falling down." The dog that was to become the spiritual 'Watchman' of the bridge was a later form of animal sacrifice. Before that, as the actions again suggest, a human sacrifice (child) was interred in the foundations of each arch, to secure stability and appease the river spirits.

An even more glaring example is given in "Oranges and Lemons" where it ends "Here comes a chopper to chop off your head - chop - chop - chop" - for the last child. ("The Devil takes the hindmost").

The purifying midsummer Need fires and sacrifice at sunrise were recalled by the children's game of passing a smouldering stick around their circle. The one left holding it when it finally went out had to pay a forfeit - originally he forfeited his life!

Between haymaking and harvest horses had a rest but children didn't. They imitated former forays of knights by riding "piggy-back" - 'pick-a-back'. Fighting from the back or shoulders of a stronger child, the 'knight' would try to dislodge or overthrow his opponent, whilst youngsters charged alongside shouting encouragement astride their hobby horses (or broomsticks).

During August the regimented rows of stooked sheaves provided an ideal playground for 'hide and seek' or battleground for 'soldiers'. When hot and tired of chasing and war games their mood changed to the other 'Mighty Reaper" as they portrayed funeral processions and acted out the parts for 'Poor Mary is a-weeping', 'Who killed Cock Robin' and 'Old Roger is dead'. Fortunately a child's early conception of death is a fantasy; those 'killed' in battle lived on again - after a count of fifty!

Hands and feet, fingers and toes all played a big part in teaching numerals, concentration and coordination. Tiny tots were tickled by "This little piggy went to market" and "Incy Wincy Spider". They counted without realising it by singing 'This' old man, he played one", "One man went to mow" or "Ten green bottles".

Hands and fingers got into a twist learning 'Here's the church, here's the steeple'....., and for the slightly older ones, the intriguing variety of patterns that could be made with a length of string - called "cats' cradles".

Autumn heralded games connected with the fruits of the earth. Probably the best known is "conkers", properly called "conquerors". Although it is now played pendulously with the polished mahogany coloured horse chestnut before the 18th century cobnuts were used and the victor ate the nut of the vanquished as a reward. At other seasons the game was played with live snails - but these were not usually eaten afterwards!

A stinging success were dried peas - propelled by a blast of air through hollowed elderberry sticks, but pea-shooters had a limited range. Far further reaching were acorn 'pop' guns. Acorns also provided a plentiful supply of ammunition for slings and catapults.

Chestnuts, hazel nuts and round stones (stoneys) also served as marbles (from which material the originals were made). 'Glasseys', a corruption of glass eyes, often came out of the smashed neck of mineral water bottles.

Another name was 'alleys', red ones were 'blood-alleys', ball bearings were 'steelies' and baked clay - 'knickers'. The main rule was that the marble should be flicked by the thumb whilst the third knuckle touched the ground.

'Bob Apple' at Halloween was a reminder of man's original sin in the Garden of Eden, when the serpent tempted Eve and Eve tempted Adam to eat the apple.

In the winter running about games were in demand to keep warm. Tic, Touch, Horney and He were all names given to the chaser (the devil) who tried to catch his quarry. "Touch Iron" recalled the Celtic invasion with iron weapons and "Touch Wood" the reverence for tree spirits and "Jack in the Green".

A great pre-game ritual of counting-out was always performed, until only one person was left to act as chaser. But was it all left to chance? "Eeni - meeni - miney - mo" was this an ancient method of counting to choose a sacrificial victim? Even in their innocence there's more to most children's games than meets the eye.

84 April Spring - Propagating the Species
MAN STILL FOLLOWS THE WAYS OF THE WILD

It happens to almost every living creature at some time every year, the annual urge to propagate the species and produce young. In the search for a mate, the setting up of a home and the selection of feeding grounds, Nature has evolved a pattern of precedence, which, apart from individual variations, runs with a connecting thread throughout the wide, wild world.

In our temperate zone, conception is conducted so that the offspring will be born at the most opportune time - usually Spring. To animals and birds this has the advantages of lengthening daylight, warmer weather, a rapidly increasing food supply like insects and plants, and protection from the elements - shelter and shade.

One of the most noticeable examples at the moment is the Dawn chorus. The birds wake, stretch, preen themselves and start singing. The earliest is the blackbird some 45 minutes before sunrise. Then in approximate order follow the song-thrush, pigeon, robin, mistle-thrush, dove, pheasant, warbler, wren, tit, sparrow and finch. By dawn all are singing. Brightest and best when the sun rises from a clear blue sky, but later and more subdued if it is overcast or raining - just like us!

But why do they sing? It's partly because they are in high spirits - it's good to be alive so why not sing about it; and partly a natural stimulation for sex. In the majority of species it is the males that make the most noise! The song indicates the type of bird that is singing, its sex, condition, position of its nesting area, the site of its feeding grounds and size of its territory.

The song echoes beyond the boundaries and warns all approaching males that the territory is already taken and any intruder will be tackled - they must find another site. To the females the song suggests "Here I am, have me." When successful it arouses their curiosity, draws their attention, increases their adulation, and as they come closer, it excites their sexual response.

Some birds continue calling all day and may repeat their request more than a thousand times between dawn and nightfall; others rest around midday and resume again in the evening.

Roosting proceeds in roughly the reverse order of the Dawn chorus. Thus the first to awaken and sing are the last to be silent and sleep. Starlings, robins, pheasants and blackbirds almost invariably give their last call as they are flying to their roost.

Birds sing by inherited instinct. Additions and variations on that theme are learnt later. It has also been discovered that they have regional dialects! By differing the pitch and rhythm they court their future companions. They not only raise the alarm but also distinguish between airborne or grounded predators. By listening to the calls I can often tell where our cats are prowling. It is a consequence of the need for survival that although every species sings a different song their alarm calls are similar and recognised by all.

The highest notes come from the song of the wren, with a frequency of 4,000 cycles per second equivalent to the top notes of a piano. Its melody is so fast that it covers ten notes every second and is virtually unintelligible to the human ear unless slowed down on a tape recorder. At the opposite end of the scale the lowest notes come from the 'booming' bittern, who resides in the reeds. Like a foghorn it can be heard three miles away!

Many birds are known, named or nicknamed after the sound they make. The lapwing cries "Pee-wit". "A little bit of bread and no cheese" says the yellow hammer and of course there are the calls of the "chiff- chaff" and the "cuckoo".

Some birds mimic others, and especially adept at this is the starling. I was well and truly fooled whilst gardening one Friday morning - Good Friday - and April the first. I heard the twittering of a swallow on the branch above only to discover it was a starling.

I felt a proper April fool. They can also mimic the tones of our telephone accurately - and embarrassingly!

The dominant singing of the cock bird ensures that his eventual mate accepts the size and boundaries of his territory when she joins him. The feeding site has to be large enough to provide a sufficient amount of food to feed the chicks - without wasting excessive time and energy on the wing! There may be several other species breeding in the area but they do not compete for the same food, nesting material or space.

Thrushes and blackbirds require a good supply of worms, tits like caterpillars, swallows and martins, flies, moths and mosquitoes, rooks and jackdaws, grain and grubs.

Their nests are made from different materials, old grasses and stems, mosses and feathers, mud and sticks. They are sited in bushes, tiny hollows in trees, under eaves and in the tree tops.

Ground feeders gather grain, grubs and worms. Some species scavenge bushes, branches and bark for insects and spiders, whilst others soar gathering mouthfuls of morsels on the wing. Which is why they can all live so close together in harmony.

Some stay on the same territory throughout the year and only bother to defend it during the breeding season (with the exception of the robin!)

But should an intruder dare to challenge ownership the song cycle becomes more rapid, agitated and harsh, if the adversary comes nearer both birds start to hop and jump excitedly. Feathers are fluffed up to make themselves look bigger. Crests stiffen and plumage markings are exposed in a dazzling display of colours. It's a case of avoidance rather than violence, it is the intruder who submits. With.drooped head and wings he turns and flies away. Otherwise a short, sharp skirmish takes place, the nearer the nest the fiercer the fight for the owner has most to lose. Gulls battle with their bills, pigeons with their wings and game birds with their spurs, but seldom is much damage done or blood spilled. The vanquished slinks away to find another site whilst the victor proclaims his triumphal song all the louder.

Once birds are suitably paired and sited there is little competition from rivals for they, too, are settling down. This compels the pairs to spend more time together. And because intrusions are less likely not so much singing is required and more time is devoted to building the nest, to "woo" and to "bill and coo".

They cosset one another especially around the head and neck, and by so doing preen the parts that the other cannot reach. Finally comes fertilisation. This can happen anything from once to ten times daily during the egg producing period.

My gardening was interrupted by the quacking and splashing of a mallard (duck) in the nearby river. Her affections were being sought by three drakes at the same time. They nearly drowned her with their desires, but happily she has now found her match and was last seen waddling off towards the mill pool with her drake following in hot pursuit, while the two unsuccessful contestants wander along the meandering stream in search of other conquests.

Although seabirds colonise for safety at breeding times, flocks of land birds disperse into scattered pairs to make it more difficult for predators to inflict heavy losses.

When incubation begins either the pair take it in turns to sit on the nest, or the female sits, and sometimes the male brings her food. In reality she is training him ready to feed the young! In other cases she does everything and he does nothing - except to keep on crowing about it!

But it is not only birds that exhibit this annual pattern of behaviour. Animals do it their way. The stag announces the autumn rut by constantly roaring from his vantage point. He hopes that hinds will be forthcoming to establish his harem - their calves will be born in the springtime. Trees are flayed and any assailant who answers his challenge is assaulted with his antlers. Though frequently some subordinate male may lure the hinds away while the aggressors are locked in combat.

Dog foxes and vixens utter their spine chilling eerie yelping bark during courtship rituals which start in January. Bulls roar, dogs howl, and constant caterwauling causes many a shoe or slipper to be thrown at the contestants from the bedroom window!

However, all use a similar method of marking their territories. Instead of patrolling them regularly they maintain their mandate by leaving scented markers of urine or faeces, sometimes called 'spraints'. These animal notice boards advertise the extent of the boundaries and also convey messages of condition and readiness to mate. They are added to by the female and used as a means of communication. Animals can detect minute changes in the concentrations so passed, and my bull always used to sniff his cows as they urinated. If one was coming into season his nose would wrinkle and make his copper bull ring stand on end, a sure sign that the cow would be served before the day was out.

Our Doberman dog used the small conifers that dotted our garden as markers - to such an extent that most have since died. That is one advantage of lamp posts!

Rabbits have a facial gland with which they 'chin' sticks, and cats love to be fondled around the head and back as it passes their scent onto others.

Almost invariably the males range further afield in the breeding season end keep infiltrating neighbouring patches. It must be borne in mind that territory can only be held for as long as the individual can successfully defend it which is nature's way of weeding out those who are growing old and weak, and maintaining the survival of the fittest.

In reading this do you recognise the close comparisons between the ways of the wild and our own actions? Isn't it the males who make the most noise and travel the furthest over their stomping ground? Are not our boundaries also marked - by deeds and documents, barbed wire, prickly hedges and notices such as "Private", "Keep Out" or "Trespassers Will Be Prosecuted"?

Bill & Coo

Don't we say that courting couples "peck and pet", "bill and coo", "act like a couple of lovebirds" and use scents, shampoos and aftershave to enhance their odour and hopefully encourage adoration Isn't combat between suitors more often a verbal show of strength rather than muscular action?

Although we flock together for games, dances and work, spouses really like to be left alone together and privacy in the eventual nest is jealously guarded by bolts and bars, curtains and blinds. Then, when it finally comes down to feeding the family, isn't it still the female that does most of the maternal work while he can't stop crowing about it? To my mind it's not a case of going back to nature - we've never left it!

85 May Hair Care
HAIR-RAISING TALE OF THE UNFAITHFUL WIFE

When you were young were you encouraged to eat up all your crusts with the inducement that it would make your hair curl? I was and I used to wonder - who wants curly hair anyway? Still I ate up all my crusts, mainly because as a growing lad I was perpetually hungry (probably a sign of worms!) yet my hair has always remained straight.

There are so many fallacies, fables, sayings and stories about our hair that perhaps you might like to be reminded of some of them.

It was once widely thought that long hair on a man denoted great strength and that when his hair was cut his strength diminished until it grew again. That was the basis behind the biblical story of Samson. What a load of rubbish! His weakness was caused by his passion for Delilah!

Another assumption was that free and luxuriant growth gave vigour and vitality whilst lank and straight hair signified a sly and cunning person. Curls symbolised pride, cheerfulness and serenity. A red head was the sure sign of a fiery temper but perhaps of more importance - a passionate disposition in love.

Because most of our invaders were red-headed Danes or blond Angles it was always a dark-haired young man who brought the best luck 'first footing' across the threshold to let in the New Year.

In women long flowing hair has always been considered a great beauty especially if it was curly or wavy. Celtic girls wore their hair loose around their shoulders until they married, when, to signify their new status, it was plaited. Should any wife be found guilty of infidelity she was tied to the courtroom's wooden wall with her plaits fastened out above her head. From a set distance her husband then had to decide whether to sever the plaits with his throwing axe and take her back, or aim lower and terminate the marriage.

After the last war mock courts punished continental women who had collaborated with the enemy by cutting off their hair. And prisoners most of the world over were subjected to the humiliation of having their head close cropped or shaved to aid detection should they escape.

The lengths to which some men have gone to try to cure their baldness is unbelievable. Here the countryman scored handsomely over his city cousins. For at least all the ingredients necessary were readily at hand and most were free of charge. They included a compress of cowpats - or a poultice of poultry manure. To sleep in a cap of bruised ivy leaves. To rub nettle juice on nightly. Another rather sticky solution was to rub the head with a raw onion until it became red, then smear it with honey (the head, not the onion).

For those whose 'thatch' was wearing thin, the old advice was to have it cut on a waxing moon, for then it would soon grow again. Although if it were cut on a waning moon it would stay short longer and so save the expense of having it cut as often!

Blacksmith s scissors

In the countryside the blacksmith often ran a successful sideline doubling up as the village barber. It was because he knew how to keep his razor, clippers and scissors well sharpened on his cranked grinding stone, so that they cut instead of plucked the hairs from the head. The routine was usually the same. Gradually a group of men and youngsters gathered, each took it in turn to sit on the folded sack on the anvil. A basin of about the correct size was inverted onto the head, all below the rim was clipped or shaved away. The hair that remained when the bowl was removed was then roughly shortened to about an inch. Working men were not fussy what it looked like since it was covered with a cap or billy-cock hat for most of the time.

The other person who often performed haircutting was the shepherd. He was in constant practice daggling his sheep and therefore very handy with his sharp sheep shears. His style tended to taper the hairline, without the use of a basin.

There were many superstitions about cutting hair. One was, "Better never be born than Sunday shorn." Another that all hair clippings had to be swept up and burnt or a witch might steal them and therefore gain control over you as she would have your vibrations. And again - if the hairs were thrown to the winds, birds would weave them into their nests, causing the donor excruciating headaches.

In the mid 1600's the followers of King Charles I were called Royalists or Cavaliers. They wore their hair long. Their opponents, the Puritans under the leadership of Oliver Cromwell, had their's close-cropped which is why they gained the nickname of "Roundheads".

When the monarchy was restored under Charles II, many Puritans wished to hide their previous strict loyalties but were unable to do so because of their lack of hair. To conceal their shortcomings they took to wearing wigs. Because these 'periwigs' or 'perukes', as they were also called often enhanced their features, it rapidly became a fashion. At first wigs were widely condemned by the church but soon even clergymen were wearing them.

Wigs were worn by all classes. The best, made from human hair, cost over £200 in those days; some of horsehair less than £2. Grey was the most popular colour, black the least. The more important the person the bigger the wig. Hence the expression "bigwig". They are still worn today by the Lord Chancellor, the Speaker and judges.

The fighting forces had a special 'campaign' wig and there are many accounts of men charging into battle losing their wig on the way and facing the enemy baldheaded. Most popular were 'pigtail' wigs - either tied up in a knot or hung down the back. Because they were greased with lard or animal fat they marked the uniform. So special deep backed collars were designated for protection - which sailors still wear! In 1804 the length of the forces 'pigtail' was reduced to seven inches and in 1808 it was cut off altogether.

Soon natural hair was in fashion again but by the 1850s it was strictly short back and sides to reduce the infestations of vermin, but wigs have left us with other legacies both in our dress and in our language. Long wigs hid the wide white collar then in use. The only pieces that could be seen were the two front edges. To economise on washing, false fronts containing these two white strips were used. When wigs went out of fashion the two white "bands" continued to be worn by Canons of the C of E and non-conformist ministers on their black Geneva gowns. And they, too, can be seen to this day.

Ladies also wore wigs, some very high, like beehives with curls at the front. Others - ringlets of false hair which surrounded the face - were called "heartbreakers". Because heads were bald, shaved or close cropped under the wig, special night wigs or night caps came into widespread use to keep the head warm in bed.

To gain extra revenue a tax of one guinea was imposed in 1795 on all wealthy people who powdered their hair. Those who paid up and continued the practice were henceforth known as "guinea-pigs". About the same time a succession of bad harvests caused the forces to curtail their annual use of 7,500 tons of flour for wig powdering and turn it into bread instead!

Before photography was invented young men who travelled carried a 'locket' containing a lock of their sweetheart's hair as a memento.

During Victorian times hair was smoothed with macassar oil, which unfortunately stained the fabric of chairs and settees. So special linen or lace covers were made to put over the headresting parts - "ANTI- macassars"!

Hair has played an important part in other religions and countries too. Moslems had a single tuft left to enable Mohammed to draw them up to Paradise. The North American Indians had a 'scalp lock' that was removed at death to allow the soul to escape from the body. When Manchu invaded and conquered China they found the people so slippery to catch that the Chinese were required (until 1912) to wear a plaited pig tail as a sign of servitude and make them easier to arrest.

But back to Britannia; before the permanent wave or "perm", ladies made temporary improvements by rolling their hair in paper or rag curlers at night, or wrapping it around rollers hidden under a headscarf by day. Curling tongs heated in the fire and first tested against scorching on a sheet of brown paper put crinkles and curls into many a straight strand before a dance on a Saturday night - sadly only too soon to return to its original state if it was raining outside.

Space prevents me from mentioning further, about singeing after cutting to seal the ends, hydrogen peroxide blondes, purple tints, top knots and buns, pony tails, crew cuts and DA's, hairpins, hairnets and snoods, or the sayings "Not turn a hair", "Stop splitting hairs", "Keep you hair on" and "Let your hair down", and one which is starting to affect me - "white hair is a sign of age not wisdom"!

However I did come across some excellent advice on hair-care in an old nursery book. It states: "To calm an unruly child gently brush its hair; if this does not work use the other end of the brush on the other end of the child."

But as you all know, such a method of controlling misbehaviour in young children is now beyond the pale - and the law. It's enough to make your hair "stand on end", isn't it.

In the fairy tale, Rapunzel, the fair maiden, who was imprisoned in the castle tower, let down her wealth of golden tresses to allow her suitor to climb up to her! Assuming that her hair grew at an average rate of six inches per year, it must have been an extremely low tower or a very tall story! Alternatively she may have been a rather old maid!